DAY OF THE DAWG

DAY OF THE DAWG

A FOOTBALL MEMOIR

HANFORD DIXON

WITH RANDY NYERGES

GRAY & COMPANY, PUBLISHERS
CLEVELAND

Gray & Company, Publishers
www.grayco.com

Library of Congress Cataloging-in-Publication Data
Dixon, Hanford
Day of the dawg : a memoir / Hanford Dixon with Randy Nyerges.
p. cm.
ISBN 978-1-59851-092-8
1. Dixon, Hanford, 1958- 2. Football players—United States—Biog-raphy. 3. Cleveland Browns (Football team : 1946-1995) I. Nyerges, Randy. II. Title.
GV939.D58A3 2012
796.357092—dc23
[B]
2012022982

Printed in the United States of America
1

To my parents, kids, and Bud Holmes

Contents

CHAPTER ONE

Dawn of the Dawgs

The heat and humidity were stifling. Who could believe that just five months ago these same Lake Erie breezes, now vainly attempting to spread some relief from the eye-stinging sweat, callously dumped mountains of snow on these very grounds?

It was training camp for the 1984 Cleveland Browns. My fourth year in the NFL already.

We had just missed the playoffs the year before. We slugged out a victory over the goddamn Pittsburgh Steelers in the final game of the 1983 season, featuring a Jack Lambert ejection as he clobbered Brian Sipe on the sideline right in front of our bench. Maybe he was trying to even the score for Joe "Turkey" Jones's backflip pile-driving of Terry Bradshaw in 1976. While a victory over the Steelers is always sweet, we then got the bad news that we had missed the playoffs on a tiebreaker.

Brian had been lured away by a pile of Donald Trump cash to the New Jersey Generals of the United States Football League. Southern Cal golden boy Paul McDonald, who had patiently caddied for Brian for four years, put down his clipboard, untangled his headset from his Paul McCartney hairdo and took the helm. Terry Nugent and Tom Flick competed for the backup spots. They had some fine wide receivers to throw to as well.

The Browns' defense over the previous few years had had some issues with pressuring the quarterback. And as we scrimmaged that day, McDonald and company were rifling the ball through the thick August air with ease. I called out to our defensive linemen to get some pressure on them. Of course, we didn't hit quarterbacks during practice—too many dollars and blow-dried hairstyles were at stake. But we needed to get on those guys. We needed to get into their heads. In the NFL, an ordinary quarterback can look pretty good if he gets enough time to throw. And a good quarterback can become very ordinary if someone like a snarling Mark Gastineau is in his face sucking the air out of the quarterback's nose.

I quickly flashed back to my boyhood days in Theodore, Alabama. I remembered seeing a dog chase a cat down Simpson Lane, the dirt road that led to my house. "Look, guys," I told the defensive linemen between plays, "if you can't get at these guys, then what the hell are Bradshit and Fouts going to do to us? (Never mind that Bradshaw had just retired.) Think of the QB like he's a cat, and you're a dog. The dog needs to catch the cat."

We lined up for another play.

"He's the cat, you're the dog. Don't let him get away," I shouted as I retreated to my right cornerback position. Then to help them remember, I let out a few barks. We ran the play, and then before the next play, I let out a few more barks. Pretty soon, it was a matter of routine. It was to let the linemen know they were like dogs, and they were to catch the cat.

Fans regularly attend preseason practice there at Lakeland Community College in Kirtland, Ohio, about a half-hour's drive east of Cleveland. One of the first things I noticed after my arrival in Cleveland in 1981 was how crazy and obsessive Cleveland Browns fans are. Yes, other teams have very strong and loyal fan bases across the country, but here in Cleveland the fans are just sheer nuts. The Browns dominated the local sports scene. They had dominated the NFL in the 1950s, and because of the many lean years by the Cleveland Indians and, later on, the Cleveland Cavaliers, Cleveland was a football city first and foremost.

It didn't take long for the fans attending practice to start barking as well. We'd line up for a play, I'd let out a few barks and the fans, sometimes thousands in attendance, began barking too. This kept on going and going throughout the couple of weeks that practices were open to the public.

Frank Minnifield had come to us from the USFL's Arizona Wranglers. He missed most of camp as legal entanglements from his transition from the Wranglers to the Browns were worked out. That probably was a good thing, too, since Frank had just played in the USFL title game a few weeks prior and was nursing an arch strain. At 5-9 and 185 pounds, Frank was not a big guy. He blew out his knee during his rookie year in the USFL. But he had guile. Gallons of it. And with his 4.4 speed, he was just a terrific one-on-one defender who could fly with the fleetest.

The barking at practice continued during training camp. The fans were really getting into it. A year passed, and just before the 1985 season, I got word that someone in the Browns' front office wanted to see me. It's not unusual to be called into the coach's office here and there, especially for a smartass troublemaker like me, but rarely do the front office people call you in. I stopped by this administrator's office, and, being the businessman that he was, he got right down to business.

"Hanford," he told me, "all this stuff about dogs and barking and everything is a distraction. We're not the Cleveland Dogs. We're the Cleveland Browns. We don't have a logo on our helmets, and we're not about to. And we already have a mascot."

Yeah. A sexually ambiguous, pointy-eared fairy in a stocking cap. Over the years, I'm sure it struck terror into the hearts of elf-phobics like Dick Butkus, Chuck "Concrete Charlie" Bednarik, and Mean Joe Greene. Even Browns owner Art Modell hated that emblem and actually purged it from official use in the late 1960s. But since there was nothing to replace it, it still was the closest thing the Browns had to a mascot.

"Well," I said, "I think it's kind of taken off on its own. And hey, the fans like it."

No one on the coaching staff seemed to have a problem with it. Just the pointy heads in the front office. Why would they consider it an on-field distraction if the coaches had no problem with it?

"I know," the administrator said. "But we need you to just concentrate on football. That's what we pay you for, not to lead some dog circus."

I left the meeting a bit stunned. This barking thing was stirring our defense and giving the fans something to join in with us. I told Frank about the meeting, and he had one of his usual devious solutions.

"Get your ass over to my apartment, Hanford. We'll take care of this."

I headed over to Frank's apartment after practice one day, just before our opening exhibition game of the 1985 season, against the goddamn Steelers. Frank rolled out a long blank banner and grabbed a paintbrush. We painted "Dog Pound."

"What are we going to do with that?" I asked as Michelangelofield finished his masterpiece.

"We're going to hang this in front of the bleachers before the Steelers game. We're going to call it the Dog Pound." Yes, we originally spelled it correctly, but the "Dawg" moniker evolved in the media. The first mention of the dog (still grammatically proper) phenomenon appeared in *The Cleveland Plain Dealer* on September 25, 1984.

Cleveland Stadium was a cavernous, two-deck, 80,000-plus-seat stadium built on a landfill. Originally the stadium was going to hold 100,000 seats, but cost overruns quickly required some changes, and engineers cut out 20,000 seats. Still, it was big. It was built to accommodate almost any event, from football to baseball to track, boxing, you name it. It was once even modified for a motocross event. For baseball, the center-field wall was a steroidious 470 feet away, with lower-deck box seats descending to field level. That might be OK for baseball, but that created many sight obstructions for football. Posts and pillars supported a roof, but again those posts obstructed the view for many otherwise good seats in both decks. On the east end of the stadium was a separate section made up of benches—the bleachers. Even though the view was unobstructed, these were definitely the cheap seats. Well into the 1970s, you could watch a Cleveland Indians game from the bleachers for 50 cents. These seats were often the last to be sold, and in the '60s and '70s, you would often find it filled with Steelers fans when they were in town. Can you imagine that now? The Dawg Pound filled with Steelers fans? It was in the bleachers where the most vocal, crazy, and, yes, intoxicated fans could be found.

The locker rooms, especially for the visiting team, were cramped and crude. In the visitors' locker room, players hung their clothes on rusty nails hammered in the concrete brick wall. The shower, which often featured no hot water, flooded the coaches' office. Ernest Givins of the Houston Oilers called it a "rat hole." Yes, but it was our rat hole.

Years later, when proposals were being considered to build a new stadium on the site, some suggested the new digs should have a dome. But that would have turned The Dawg Pound into The Poodle Parlor. That's not the way we do things in Cleveland. Football wasn't meant to be played in a sterile, climate-controlled environment on a cushy carpet with tofu and soybeans sold at the concession stand. It was meant to be played on sandy mud painted green, with blinding rain, snow, and razor-like winds whipping in off Lake Erie cutting into your icicle-dripped face.

Before each game, we were like gladiators marching to battle as we clip-clomped almost in unison over rotting floorboards and through the narrow, dank, 50-foot tunnel leading toward the field via the first base dugout used by the Indians during the summer. The same path trod by greats like Jim Brown, Otto Graham, Lou Groza, Dick Schafrath, Gene Hickerson, among other mighty towering men. If you were claustrophobic, you had a problem. But as you got closer to emerging on the other end, you heard that roar get louder and louder, until everything burst into color and an earsplitting roar as we ascended the dugout steps. That scene repeated before every game, exhibition or conference championship, good season or bad.

Before that exhibition game against those goddamn Pittsburgh Steelers, Frank and I hung the banner in front of the bleachers. It didn't take long for the fans in the bleachers to assume the role. They continued the barking, and even though the game was a bust, the Dawg Pound was born. It has outlasted other phenomena of the past, such as the Rams' Fearsome Foursome or the Vikings' Purple People Eaters or the Steelers' Steel Curtain.

"We sic 'The Dogs' on the quarterbacks," safety Al Gross told *The Plain Dealer*.

"A dog takes very little from anybody when he's ferocious," linebacker Eddie Johnson said. "That's what we wanted to instill in our defensive line. In order for us to be successful, our defensive line has to play like dogs." Eddie was known as "The Assassin," but in the locker room, we called him "Bullethead." His close-shaven head was shaped like a bullet, and he had no neck.

Years later, for some reason I just don't know, Eddie claimed he was the originator of the Dawg phenomenon. Sadly, Eddie died in January 2003 of colon cancer at the age of 43. More on that later.

As the season progressed, the fans not only barked, they began to dress the part. Every week, there were new dog masks, dog noses, bone-shaped hats, and other crazy costumes. They usually brought in a doghouse, which took three or four guys to carry in but took only one to carry out. The phenomenon kept growing, and even though it was a difficult season for the Browns, the Dawg Pound was now a part, a big part, of this storied franchise.

Around the locker room, we called each other "Dawg." When the Browns played the Eagles in an exhibition game in London, I remember getting quite an odd look from the doorman of the hotel when I asked him, "Whassup, Dawg?" It was Dawg this, Dawg that. To this day, it has worked its way into the American vernacular. Why do you think Randy Jackson says, "Yo, Dawg" on *American Idol*? Every night, America would flip on *The Arsenio Hall Show* to find the Cleveland native fist-pumping to the "Woof, woof, woof" of the audience. Whenever I would return to my parents' home in Theodore, Alabama, everywhere I would go around town, I'd be greeted with, "Woof, woof, woof."

Among other business ventures, I'm a real estate broker in the Cleveland area. I got myself into some trouble recently with my dog reference when a real estate agent from another company called me for information on one of the properties I had listed for sale.

Either he wasn't a Browns fan or I wasn't thinking or, most likely, both. His name was Muhammad, thus I assume (in hindsight) that he was Muslim.

"Meestor Deexon," he said in his Apu-like accent. "I would like to show your property to one of my clients."

"Great, Dawg!" I told him. "Sell it for me."

An uncomfortable pause ensued.

"Why you call me a dog, Meestor Deexon?" Muhammad said. "I do nothing bad to you, so why you feel you must call me a dog?"

Suddenly realizing that this gentleman was not up to snuff on Cleveland Browns history, I fumbled for a save.

"Ah, oh, sorry, I just call everybody Dawg."

"Well I appreciate if you not call me a dog," he admonished me sternly. Apparently, he didn't realize that in Cleveland, it's supposed to be an honor to be addressed as "Dawg" by the Top Dawg himself.

The Dawg Pound fans quickly developed a reputation of making life difficult for opposing teams. It was bad enough for opponents to come in and deal with the shitty locker room and shittier weather, and playing on a surface exquisitely landscaped with green-painted mud. Now they also had to deal with the Dawg Pound. The worst of it would come when an opposing team had to huddle up in the end zone. The Dawg Pound was just a few feet behind them, up a small incline. Dog biscuits, batteries, beer cups, snow balls, you name it, would come whirling rapid fire out of the stands, accompanied by the loud, incessant barking.

Ultimately, the dog food and such had to be banned from the

stadium, but much contraband would still find its way in. And at least one game was decided by those crazy dawgs.

In October 1989, we were playing the Denver Broncos. John Elway was Public Enemy Number One in Cleveland, having engineered "The Drive" in the 1986 season's AFC title game, in which he led the Broncos 98 yards to a game-tying touchdown and Denver went on to beat us in overtime. In the fourth quarter of the 1989 game, the Broncos huddled in the end zone in front of the Dawg Pound, and the onslaught began. It got so bad that the referee ordered us to switch ends, resulting in us now getting the wind at our backs. Frank came up with a fumble recovery deep in our territory with two minutes left, and Bernie Kosar engineered a drive of his own to set up a 47-yard field goal by Matt Bahr as time expired. The ball barely cleared the crossbar, and the wind certainly made the winning difference.

In a 1987 Monday night game, the Dawg Pound fans were reveling in the 17-0 lead we had built on the then-Los Angeles Rams. Biscuits came flying out of the Pound, so much so that the officials asked the Browns to make an announcement on the public address system to knock it off. Talk about trying to put out a fire with gasoline! The Browns wisely declined to make such an announcement, fearing it would only egg things on. No shit, Sherlock. Two weeks later, just before a game with the Falcons, the front office people asked me to not rile up the Pound. Sure, yeah, no problem. I'll get right on that. Did they think that I'd really be able to calm them down? Did they think I even wanted to calm them down?

Even before the bleachers were known as the Dawg Pound, they still got into the act. In a 1979 game against Houston, the officials had to move an extra point attempt to the other end of the field because of the various fodder pelting the Oilers.

Just for kicks, a couple of years ago, I attended a Browns game and sat in the Dawg Pound. It didn't take more than a minute for the fans to recognize I was in their midst. One by one, they yelled and pointed. "Look, it's Hanford Dixon! Woof, woof, woof!" They barked, and I barked back at them. They barked louder and became a bit more rowdy. Before the end of the first quarter, I realized that even though they were friendly dawgs, they outnumbered me about 2,000 to 1. Imagine standing in a pen with 2,000 overly friendly mad fans in various states of inebriation starting to swoop down on you. I casually ducked away.

Calvin Hill, the former Cowboys great, finished his career with the Browns. He was the offensive Rookie of the Year way back in 1969, and his final season was my rookie year. Calvin was the consummate businessman. He always wore the nicest suits and carried a briefcase, always looking like the Yale boy he was. After his retirement, he worked for the Browns' front office. One day, he suggested something to me.

"This Dawg Pound thing has gotten pretty big," he said. "Did you ever think about trademarking it?"

I figured if Calvin suggested it, it had to be a good idea. (Years later, Steelers running back Jerome Bettis trademarked "The Bus," and New York Knicks sensation Jeremy Linn filed a trademark application for "Linsanity.") I picked up the phone and called my agent and attorney, Bud Holmes. I told him about what Calvin had suggested, and Bud agreed it would be a good thing to do, and he would get right on it.

After some time had passed, Bud gave me a call. "I've got bad news for you, Hanford," he said in his Mississippi drawl. "Dawg Pound and Top Dawg have already been trademarked."

"What? By who?"

"You won't believe it."

"Who?"

"Those terms were trademarked by NFL Properties, at the request of the Cleveland Browns."

WHAT? I couldn't believe it. The Browns told me to knock off all this dawg pound nonsense, and then they go behind my back and trademark it? I was madder than a southern copperhead tangled in barbed wire. My immediate thought was to sue, but I didn't have a case. Once it was trademarked, it was trademarked. The Browns didn't do anything fraudulent, just sleazy.

As an avid hunter and fisherman, I have plenty of stories about how the big one got away. I habitually purchased lottery tickets at a beverage store after practice. There were the occasional two-dollar winners, but of course, most of the time, these lottery tickets would turn out to be worthless. My wife Hikia, a meticulous housekeeper, once tossed out a stack of lottery tickets she assumed were duds. That evening, I find out that a big-dollar lottery ticket had been sold at the beverage store where I bought those tickets. To this day, that prize has gone unclaimed. Another big one that got away.

Tens of millions of dollars have transacted in the name of The Dawgs or Top Dawg. Neither Frank nor I ever received one nickel in royalties. Hell, Paul Brown received royalties for every nearly useless single-bar facemask stamped out in the 1950s. Talk about another big one that got away. Not to mention the three AFC title games with the Broncos. The NFL took in licensing fees all around. Hallmark even put out a Christmas card depicting Santa lounging in a chair watching a Browns game with a dog in a "Browns Dawg Pound" sweatshirt.

When the Browns moved to Baltimore in 1995, the Hawaii-Pacific Apparel Group in Honolulu successfully trademarked Top Dawg, the presumption being the Browns, who were now the Ravens, abandoned the trademark. When the expansion Browns set up shop in 1999, they tried to re-establish the trademark, but were turned down because Hawaii-Pacific now held the mark. A court battle lingered on for nearly a decade, with the Browns continuing to use the Top Dawg mark. It ended with a ruling by a U.S. District judge in New York in February 2008 that the Browns and NFL Properties were the rightful owners of the trademark. They might be the lawful owners of the trademark, but we all know who really brought everyone to the bank, only to be locked outside the front door.

In 1989, I put together a calendar featuring several of the Browns in very gentlemanly poses. I, of course, was in that calendar, but I had to refer myself as Dogg. Had I tried to refer to myself as the Top Dawg, I would have had to have paid the NFL $10,000 for the licensing fee.

Top Dawg had been outfoxed.

CHAPTER TWO

Southern Dawg

Merry Christmas to my parents: I was born December 25, 1958, to Hanzle and Marva Dixon in Mobile, Alabama. Dad was so excited about having a December 25 baby, he kept declaring, "I can't believe I've got my own sweet baby Jesus!"

I share a Christmas birthday with some notable people. Born the same day 900 miles away in Chicago in the back seat of an Oldsmobile was future baseball great Rickey Henderson. He was born to steal bases and hit baseballs. I was born to steal passes and hit wide receivers. Also born on Christmas were Hall of Fame running back Larry Csonka, former quarterback Kenny Stabler, Hall of Fame second baseman Nellie Fox, singer Jimmy Buffett, political consultant Karl Rove, and former second baseman Manny Trillo. Oh yeah, Jesus, too. He's the head of my life. Can't forget about him! I'm certainly in good company.

My friends all had two days a year to collect presents. I had just one. But Mom and Dad did their best. At no time do I recall being told, "This present covers both."

I grew up in a modest, three-bedroom home, approximately 1,400 square feet, on three-quarters of an acre with my parents and six-years-older sister Debra in Theodore, Alabama. Our town was a suburb of Mobile and about a two-hour drive from New Orleans. Yes, the deep South. Just barely a month before I was born, John Patterson was elected governor with the full backing of the Ku Klux

Klan. This man was such an ugly racist that the NAACP actually endorsed his opponent, George Wallace. Not the comedian George Wallace, *the* George Wallace. The George Wallace of, "Segregation today, segregation tomorrow, segregation forever." Looking back, I guess he really was a comedian, too.

Our house was nestled among some oak and sycamore trees on Simpson Lane, a small dirt road off Washington Boulevard. We were fortunate enough to have a window-unit air conditioner to get us through the stifling southern, steam-fried summers. Dad grew tomatoes and collard greens, and we had a fig tree. I hated figs. Dad made me pick them because he thought they were too sticky. I found them to be downright slimy. More slimy than okra.

As a youngster, I got into everything. I had to inspect it, play with it, throw it, take it apart, bang it, you name it. My father had a collection of guns, and one day, of course, I got into that. I found a gun and found a box of shells. Of course I had to find out if I could load a shell into the gun. I succeeded. Of course I didn't want my parents to find out what I did, so I tried to remove the shell. It was stuck. I tried and tried to find the way discharge it, to no avail. Finally, I came up with a brilliant idea.

"Look out, Debra," I told my sister. "I'm going to have to shoot this gun." That, of course, would eject the spent shell.

Debra shrieked in horror and ran out the door. She came back with the next-door neighbor who grabbed that gun away from me.

I also had my own BB gun. One day I thought it would be neat to use my bedroom wall for target practice. When Dad got home, I became the target of that leather belt.

We had our fair share of hurricanes blow in from the Gulf of Mexico. In 1969, Hurricane Camille took aim at the greater Mobile area. Despite the fact that Theodore is only 16 feet above sea level, Dad was determined to ride it out. Camille, one of only three Category 5 hurricanes to hit the American mainland, crashed ashore with its 170 mph winds howling. It didn't take long for Dad to realize we had to make a run for it. Like a scene out of an Irwin Allen movie, we struggled to get to the pickup truck in the yard, fighting through the horizontal rain that felt like we were walking through a giant sandblaster. We made it to the truck and to an elementary school where a shelter was set up. We returned home the next day, not sure what we would find, but our house stood there like a battle-weary titan.

*   *   *

It was a 10-minute walk to Burroughs Elementary School, which housed grades K-8. I hung with my friends Carlos King, David Parrish, Isaac Alston, John Walker, Derrick Payne, among others. I enjoyed elementary school. I particularly remember looking forward to May Day celebrations every spring. There would be several flagpoles that we would decorate with brightly colored cloth and ribbon strips.

I didn't feel I was being deprived of anything despite the fact that my school had all black kids. Even with the passage of the Civil Rights Act of 1964 and public school integration beginning in 1963, segregation was very much the order of the times, and that included Theodore.

A set of railroad tracks bisected the 12-square-mile town, and we lived on the "wrong" side of the tracks. About 25 percent of the population was black, and the most common faith was that of the Southern Baptist Convention.

I wasn't aware of the strife and turmoil that boiled around the state. Alabama was ground zero in the battle for civil rights, and history was being made every day in places like Selma, Huntsville, and Montgomery at the wrong end of the billy clubs and water hoses, all to the tune of snarling and snapping German shepherds. There was plenty of Klan activity, such as rallies and cross burnings, in the area, especially in the more rural parts. It was in Alabama that Jefferson Davis stood tall and took the oath of office as president of the Confederate States of America. A century later, George Wallace stood on the same spot, marked by a gold star, and delivered his odious signature line of hateful infamy.

*　　*　　*

My parents taught me about the importance of school, family and church. They didn't teach me to hate the haters. So although I slowly became aware of the struggles that were going on, my main concern was to do well in school and make sure I was home on time. Failing that, I would be straightened out by the business end of dad's leather belt.

Dad, a former army cook, was a strong, tough man. He was the authoritarian, and I knew not to question him. His word was law. He worked as a plant manager at National Gypsum. Debra and I had our chores and responsibilities, and we made sure they were carried out.

Years later, even though I was an All-America college football star who could bench press 325 pounds and run the 40 in 4.39 seconds, I still feared my father's righteous wrath. I was still subject to Dad's curfew and dictates.

One day, just before Dad left to work a 3-to-11 shift at the plant, he said, "Lee (he always called me Lee, my middle name), make sure that grass is cut before I get home." Yeah, sure, I thought. I was a big-time college football player, certainly bound for the NFL. I don't cut grass anymore.

Later that evening, the grass wasn't cut, and I knew Dad would soon be thundering down Simpson Lane in that classic blue Impala. But I didn't care. Debra admonished me that I'd better get it done, but that fell on deaf ears.

"Hanf, you better get it done," Debra kept telling me. Eventually her wisdom seeped in and I realized she was right. I'd better not push it. Dad was not as impressed with my semi-celebrity status as I was. I went out there in the pitch dark and fired up the mower. Debra, nine months' pregnant with her first child, came out with a flashlight, and I cut the grass by her guiding light.

Had I been derelict in my responsibilities, that belt was going to come snapping my way even though I was an NCAA big shot. And I would have stood there and taken it, that's how much respect I had for the man. Certainly, at the time, I hated the things he did to me. I yelled and screamed in protest, and called my parents freaks. But I look back at it now and realize that he was doing all he could to make me a better son, and ultimately, a better man.

Did Dad abuse me? By the literal definition, I guess you could say yes. But in retrospect, I understand why he did the things he did. And I'm a better person as a result. So much of what ails kids today can be traced not to tough parents, but apathetic parents. Too many parents are just afraid of disciplining their kids. Parents who just don't care. My dad cared. Our juvenile justice system would be far less clogged if parents, especially fathers, just took a simple yet genuine interest in the activities and interests of their kids and taught them basic respect. It makes no difference—black, white, suburban, country, ghetto—if the parents are involved, the kids just naturally do better at home and at school.

Dad, of course, instituted a curfew for me, and I, of course, had considerable trouble abiding by it. One thing I did was keep my bedroom window cracked open an inch or so in case I needed to sneak back into the house. One evening when I was 16, I was out on one of my late-night adventures and came back home past my curfew. No worries, I thought, I'd just come through my window. When I got around to the back of the house and to my window, I found it was closed. And locked. Debra had gotten up in the night, felt a cold draft and closed the window in my room. I ran over to her window and tapped. No response. I tapped again. No response again. The last thing I wanted to do was tap on the window of my parents' room. Suddenly, Debra emerged at her window.

"Quick, let me in!" I pleaded. She opened her window, and I reached around with both hands, and pulled my head through the opening.

BAM. I saw stars. BAM again. I got smacked upside the head. BAM again. There was my sweet, loving mother pummeling the sweet love of Jesus into my head, wailing away on me like a prize-fighter trying to put away his staggering opponent. I never missed my curfew again.

We attended Mt. Ararat Missionary Baptist Church in Theodore where Reverend B.J. Parker was pastor. I remember those hot summer days in church, with the ladies fanning themselves while wearing all sorts of fruit-flower-and-bird hats. I enjoyed singing and still can carry a tune fairly well to this day. I would sit in the front row and watch my mother sing in the choir. Dad would often get into it with Mom over her "shouts." That's when you feel the Holy Ghost come over you to the point you have to shout out a word from the Lord. Dad would tell Mom to cut out that silliness. "You're out of your ever lovin' mind," he would tell her. But Dad also suspected that Reverend Parker had a crush on Mom.

*   *   *

As a kid, I enjoyed playing football, baseball, and basketball with my friends. We usually played barefoot. One day we were playing football, and I went out for a pass. I caught it in stride and WHAM, I plowed into a telephone pole, face first, an obvious foreshadowing of my introduction to Earl Campbell a decade later.

We had a black-and-white TV, which pulled in all of two channels during the 1960s and into the '70s. WKRG Channel 5 was the local CBS outlet, and WALA Channel 10 the NBC affiliate. I enjoyed TV shows typical of a kid of that era, like *Star Trek*, *Lost In Space*, *The Flintstones*, *Bonanza*, *Batman*, *The Jetsons*, *Good Times*, and *The Jeffersons*. One of my favorites was *The Andy Griffith Show*. Loved it. I really loved the character Otis, the town drunk. Hysterically funny.

I also loved watching *All in the Family*. Archie Bunker was hilarious. I could see how black people could identify with *The Jeffersons* and *Good Times* or *Sanford and Son*, since probably about 95 percent of black America was struggling just to make it. I don't believe at all those shows were negatively stereotyping black America— they were entertaining and sometimes even educational comedy shows, for goodness sakes, not documentaries. I loved the battles between Archie Bunker and George Jefferson. I remember really laughing at the one adventure where Archie and George joined forces to try to keep a Puerto Rican family from moving into the neighborhood. They had to learn the hard way that diversity included everybody. Dad and I watched *Sanford and Son* together and laughed hysterically.

Dad and I also watched a lot of football. The closest NFL team was the New Orleans Saints, a team that started in the mid-'60s and languished pathetically for decades. Another popular team was the Atlanta Falcons. But my favorite was the Dallas Cowboys. Don Meredith, Roger Staubach, Too Tall Jones, Preston Pearson, Mel Renfro, Charlie Waters—coached by the stoic Tom Landry, who always dressed like he was attending a morticians' convention—those were great teams.

During the '60s and '70s, we would gather as a family around the radio anytime Muhammad Ali would fight. We lived and died with every punch. Dad was a big Muhammad Ali fan, and I became one as well. I loved Ali's brash and cocky personality. The thing was, though, that Ali could back it up. When he paraded around yapping, "I am the greatest," he proved it.

*   *   *

I played football, basketball, and baseball with my buddies like most kids do. I liked football and basketball, but I hated baseball. For some reason, I was just afraid of that ball. As we got older, we got stronger and faster. Eventually, it became clear that I was a bit faster than my friends. Eventually, it was obvious that I was much faster than my friends. Everywhere I went, I ran. "Slow down, boy!" my mother would constantly admonish me.

The first test of my speed came when I was about 8 years old, on a bath night. My parents ordered me to take a bath. I started filling the tub and then got distracted by something in my room. Next thing I knew, the soapy water was cascading over the tub and onto the floor. Buck naked, survival instinct took over. I bolted out the door and kept on running, Forrest Gump-style. I didn't know where I was headed, but I knew I had to get outta there. I had to go somewhere, anywhere, but back home. Eventually I realized there was nowhere for me to go. I had to go home and face my father, who was there waiting for me. I knew what was coming, and it came.

When I started ninth grade at Theodore High School, I knew I wanted to play football. But Dad had other ideas for me.

"No way in hell are you playing football," he declared. "You've got schoolwork to do, and nothing is going to interfere with that."

At great peril to my person, I decided to defy him and report to practice. I knew I was good at this game, and I had ideas of starting on the varsity as a freshman. So when I didn't come home from school on time the next day, Dad was seething. That damn belt came flying and didn't miss. But I was determined to play football, so I went to practice the next day. Same story when I got home. I would walk home from school after football practice with some of my friends and would come up with all sorts of creative excuses to keep them from actually stopping by my house. Dad didn't care who was there or what we were doing. If it was time for the belt, it was time for the belt. My friends eventually figured out that I was lying, but there was nothing I could do about that. Thank God for the soothing words of a sweet mother, whose intervention and logic prevented the next Sherman's March to the Sea.

"Oh Hanzle," Mom reasoned. "Let Hanford give it a try. We'll keep on him to make sure he's up on his work."

Dad demurred but reluctantly agreed. He came to a couple of practices to see if I really was any good. After a while, though, he began to show up at practice a bit more regularly and liked what he saw. I was playing with the big boys, not just keeping up with them but knocking them around. The football coach met with Dad and explained that I had tremendous ability and there was a potential long-term future in the game for me. I started off on the freshman team but was soon moved up to the varsity, starting at running back and defensive back. I soon adopted Muhammad Ali's brash tone and style.

I lettered in football, basketball, and track. But I wound up quitting track. I liked running the short stuff, such as the 100- or 440-yard dash. I was also on the 440-yard relay team. But the coach wanted me to run the longer stuff. I just couldn't handle that, so I gave it up after my junior year. I was a two-time conference MVP defensive player. I also returned kicks.

God gave me physical ability, but confidence is an important factor for a cornerback. I played on the varsity team when I was in the ninth grade, and I knew I would turn pro. My friends laughed, but I knew. I told my parents over and over that someday I would play for the Dallas Cowboys. They laughed, too. But I truly believed it.

*   *   *

I was a decent student—I guess I did enough to get by. I didn't enjoy school, but I didn't hate it either. I knew I had to get through it, and knowing my parents' attitude toward school, I kept my hand on the plow.

During the early to mid-'70s, desegregation was slowly working its way through the South. There were several incidents at our school, but I can't blame one group or the other. A minority of kids on both sides stirred up trouble just for the sake of stirring up trouble. There were several race riots at our high school, maybe seven or eight while I was there. And these weren't just pushing and shoving and name-calling incidents. Some kids threw rocks and bricks at each other, others brought knives. Several kids were cut. I can't say one side or the other was instigating. There were hard core kids on both sides who were just looking for trouble.

I had a cousin who kept getting in the middle of all the commotion, but I steered clear of it. I had white friends and black friends, and tended to hang with the athletic crowd. One day there was some racial ruckus going on, and there was a rumor that someone came out of a house and fired a shot at some of the black kids. Dad showed up at school in his old pickup truck to drive me home. I was glad to see him and jumped into the cab. But he then proceeded to drive around and around about four times, hoping this guy would come out. There on the floorboard was Dad's shotgun. He was calm, stern, and fearless on the ride home. I was scared shitless.

*   *   *

Theodore's football coach at that time was Thomas Carl. Coach Carl was a tough, no-nonsense coach. He expected the best of you on the field and in the classroom. He was good friends with Spencer Adams, who owned an insurance agency in Mobile. Spencer was a very active University of Southern Mississippi alum. He walked up and introduced himself to me.

"Hanford, we'd love to have you come to our university," he said.

Soon after my junior year, I began to get all sorts of letter from schools like Alabama, Auburn, and pretty much all the Southeastern Conference schools. They told me that they were watching me. Back home, Spencer began to befriend my parents. This is a common technique used to recruit athletes. There is an old saying that "the way to a man's heart is through his stomach." The way to recruit an athlete is through his parents. Ohio State's Woody Hayes was the master of this art. Although prone to colorful outbursts and obscenity-laced rants on and off the field, Woody was the smoothest when it came to living room manners. The late, great Jack Tatum, who in his nine years with the Oakland Raiders and one season with the Houston Oilers became one of the most devastating hitters in the history of the game, came home one day while still in high school and found Woody Hayes in the kitchen of his squalid

Passaic, New Jersey, apartment, chatting with his mother about banana cream pie recipes.

"My mother went on to explain her secret recipe," Jack wrote in his infamous and controversial best seller, *They Call Me Assassin*. "Woody stuffed his mouth with another piece of pie and listened. I got the feeling he had come in from Columbus to visit my mother, and the way she was talking to him made it seem like they were lifelong friends. After five or ten minutes, I couldn't see any sense in my leaning on the back of my mother's chair and listening to their conversation. They didn't need me in the room, so I left. To my surprise, no one missed me."

Other schools tried the good, old-fashioned, American method of offering Tatum cars, women, and under-the-table money. But Woody knew how to really recruit.

Browns great Dick Schafrath told of a similar recruiting visit from Woody. Dick was one of the anchors on the great Browns offensive line of the 1960s that opened holes for Hall of Famers Jim Brown, Bobby Mitchell, and Leroy Kelly. Schafrath also should be in the Hall.

"He arrived at the farm the next Sunday," Dick wrote in his book *Heart of a Mule*. "He went to church with the whole family and helped Mom cook lunch. He spent time with Dad at the barn talking about the chickens, pigs, and cows. He never said a word to me. Two hours later, he shook hands with Dad, kissed Mom on the cheek, and drove out the driveway. I came into the house a short time later and said, 'Boy, Mom, I'm not very impressed with Woody Hayes and Ohio State.' Mom looked at me, pounded her fist on the table and said, 'That's OK, Dick, you're going to Ohio State!' "

Woody never came to Theodore to try his irresistible charm on Mom and Dad. Spencer showed a demonstrable true interest in my future, and it was clear he wasn't just using my parents to get to me. Establishing that trust and confidence with my parents was the most secure way to ward off other, bigger, schools, such as Auburn or Alabama. Spencer drove me to visit USM's 1000-plus-acre campus, located in Hattiesburg, Mississippi, about two hours from my house. I met Bobby Collins, the head coach, and Jim Weatherford, the defensive back coach. They showed me the facilities, and I came away feeling this was the right fit. I wasn't concerned that the Golden Eagles had just come off an abysmal season, starting off 0-8 and finishing 3-8. I also came away believing that I was going to start my freshman year.

Coach Collins had a philosophy, or call it a technique, where he would draw a 300-mile radius circle around Hattiesburg and pursue the best talent within that boundary. It was physically easier to recruit, would be easy for families to come see the games, and was a part of the country that was rich with talent.

Back in Theodore, Spencer had Coach Carl hide my films. He didn't want any other school to even have a look at me. Coach Collins stopped by a few times as well. Not long after, Coach Carl got the call, making it official. I was offered a full-ride scholarship to the University of Southern Mississippi. After I signed my letter of intent, Spencer introduced me to an attorney, Bud Holmes. Bud had represented Walter Payton, and later, he would represent me.

CHAPTER THREE

College Dawg

"What's wrong with you, boy?" my Uncle Buddy hounded me. "Have you lost your ever-lovin' mind?"

Uncle Buddy was determined that I should attend Alabama and play for Bear Bryant. While playing for a big-name school had its appeal, I felt a sense of loyalty to USM because they had been there since day one. It just felt right. Plus I felt my chances of becoming a starter right away were better at USM.

It was August 1977. There aren't many places hotter or more humid on Earth than southern Mississippi that time of year. Starting college life was tough because I no longer had Mom and Dad to make sure I got up and got to where I had to go. I was now on my own. It took some doing and discipline, but eventually, I got in line. I was still pretty much a kid at heart, and very much a mama's boy; I called Mom every chance I could. Before I left for school, Mom gave me a Bible with my name embossed on it.

"Always keep God first in your life, and everything else will work out," Mom told me, paraphrasing Matthew 6:33: "Keep ye first the kingdom of God, and all these things shall be added unto you." I believed it then, but I believe that so much more today. There were times that I didn't put God first, and I (and others) paid a heavy price. But when I have my priorities in line, yes, things do fall into line. I still have that Bible and cherish it dearly.

I lived in Van Hall, the athletic dorm. Mom wasn't there to neatly place my plate in front of me and take it away when I was done. I had to learn to wait to eat. Dorm life was crazy. We pretty much got away with anything. Some of the guys were smoking pot. I thought that was crazy. But as a freshman, you kept your mouth shut and went about your business.

My roommate was Ronald Taylor, an undersized-but-still-stocky sophomore linebacker we called Clump. Somehow, someone found out about my ophidiophobia—the fear of snakes. The guys got a small rubber snake and positioned it in my room so that when I woke up, all I could see were those two beady little eyes looking straight at me. That little motherfucker looked like he was about to sink his fangs into my eyeball. I was so damn scared, I jumped up and tore out of that room and down the hall, surely establishing a new 40-yard dash world record. Of course Clump and the guys stood there bent over in laughter.

Although I was a mere freshman, I brought along my Muhammad Ali attitude. I made it abundantly clear that I was going to be a starter as a freshman. That didn't sit very well with the upperclassmen, and in fact, they held a meeting about what to do about me. After that meeting, one of the senior defensive ends, Reggie Odom, stood in the hall outside my dorm room and said menacingly to me, "Listen, you puny freshman, you best keep your fuckin' mouth shut. We're tired of the little shit coming from a little shit like you."

I revved up all my 160 pounds and charged after this behemoth. He reached up with one of his massive arms and flicked me aside, laughing. That of course only made me madder. I charged him again, same result. Still determined, I went at him one more time. He casually tossed me like a salad, and I realized this was a no-win situation. Reggie and his buddies laughed and walked away. But I'm the one who had the last laugh. Within a few weeks, I had indeed become the starter and wound up on the field for more snaps than any defensive player that year. In my first game, against Troy State on September 3, I snagged my first collegiate interception, which was key to our season-opening win. Later that year, in a game at Hawaii, we led, 28-26, as Hawaii lined up to kick a game-winning 27-yard field goal.

"I'll take care of this," I said in the huddle before the play. I blocked that field goal to seal the win. I finished my freshman year with 44 tackles, a pair of interceptions, and eight "big plays" (as decided by the coaches). We had big Southeastern Conference wins over Auburn, Ole Miss, and Mississippi State. I wore number 19, the same number I had in high school.

Coaches and scouts from other teams took notice of my speed and cover ability, and many of them figured the best way to beat me was to throw in someone else's direction. (This was a precursor of what was to come in the NFL.) Thus, in my four years, I picked off only nine passes.

We were known as "The Nasty Bunch," but not for the reason you might think. Yes, we played hard and nasty, but there was a small group of guys, such as Thad Dillard and J.J. Stewart, who got so worked up before a game that they would puke on the field during warm-ups. Thad played nose tackle, which meant he lined up over the ball. He'd be so worked up that several times he puked on the ball just before the center could get his hands on it. Now that's nasty.

The Mississippi Senate adopted Concurrent Resolution Number 543 in 2005 congratulating me on my career with the Golden Eagles along with the contributions of the "Nasty Bunch." While the boys and I appreciated the recognition, I don't think those senators really understood what that meant.

There were several fraternities I could have pledged, but I decided to pledge Alpha Phi Alpha. They seemed like an intelligent group of guys, nice and low key. APA was the first black fraternity, started at Cornell University in 1906. Martin Luther King, Jr. was a member, as well as W.E.B. DuBois, Jesse Owens, Thurgood Marshall, and Andrew Young.

When you pledge APA, you are assigned a big brother. My big brother was Clump. As a pledge, I was, well, I was Clump's bitch.

Every day, I had to go up to Clump and ask if there was something
I could do to serve him. Whatever he wanted, I got for him. If he
wanted something to eat, I ran down to the cafeteria and got it for
him. If it was supposed to be hot, it had better be hot. If it was supposed to be cold, it had better be cold, or I'd have to run the mission
again. We put on pledge shows, and we had to perform "steps" in
a line. I was called "Ape." That meant I led the line. I have no idea
if any of those distinguished alumni were ever the Ape, but that
would be a funny sight. If one of us screwed up, we all had to repeat
the steps. One little pledge, who we called "Light Bread," always got
us into trouble. Not only did we end up having to repeat things like
the steps, we also got paddled and forced to eat nasty foods. We
took it in stride, though nowadays many such practices and rituals are banned. Actually, it was fun. But it wasn't fun when our big
brothers took us out to the football field at midnight, made us lie
down on our backs, and fed us onions and raw eggs.

"Open up," a brother would say with a sly smile. He'd pour the
egg in your mouth and then add the onion. "I want the whole thing
swallowed." I can't tell you how many raw eggs and onions I ate,
and to this day, I can't stand onions on anything. I wonder if Thurgood Marshall developed a similar aversion.

One last thing we had to do was cross the burning sands. They
set up a patch of sand, about 10 yards wide. We had to walk barefoot through the scorching hot sand and show no emotion. If we
showed any angst or sign of discomfort, we had to start over. One
by one, we crossed those sands into the awaiting embrace of what
were now our brothers for life, where we pledged "Manly Deeds,
Scholarship, and Love for All Mankind." All the initiations, all the
errands I ran for Clump, all those terrible onions were the price I
had to pay, and to this day, I maintain that it was worth it. We knew
that once we completed the initiation it would be our turn to be big
brothers.

I chose business administration as my major but switched to
athletic administration my sophomore year. I did enough to get by,

but I didn't put as much effort into it as I should have, especially when it became clear I was headed to the NFL. And let's just say Bud and Spencer were like dads to me away from home.

One thing that I would stress to any kids, athlete or not, is to pay attention to your studies more than I did. I stress that today whenever I talk to kids. Athletes make the same mistakes as the average person. If you were a star athlete in those days, the professors, well, let's say they gave you a little love. There is still so much that I could and should have picked up in school that I had to learn the hard way. Nowadays, there is at least an emphasis on the academic wellbeing of athletes, but issues still are there. When you have college students, supposedly high school graduates, ask instructors, "What is long division?" or can't tell the difference between a vowel and consonant, then something's out of whack.

Coach Collins came over from the University of North Carolina in 1975. He was a throwback-style coach. He believed in playing great defense, great special teams and not making many mistakes on offense. We ran the ball probably 60 to 70 percent of the time. The year before I came on, the Golden Eagles started the season 0-8 but rallied to win their last three. Big recruitments like me, Clump, running back Ben "Go-Go" Gary, Stoney Parker, who is now a retired highway patrolman, and quarterbacks Jeff Hammond and Reggie Collier helped turn the program around.

After the 1981 season, Coach Collins left USM, took over the coaching duties at Southern Methodist University and got caught up in one of the most unfortunate scandals in college football history. Several players were being paid to play, and SMU was given the "death penalty"—the football program was shut down for a season. All of the players were given complete releases, thus they could play at any other school without forfeiting any eligibility. The SMU program has never been the same since. Coach Collins, after compiling a record of 43-14-1, resigned and sadly has never coached a game since. He was a tough coach but a nice man.

Coach Weatherford, on the other hand, could be downright

brutal. In fact, he almost forced me out of football. One day during practice in my freshman year, we were going through some agility drills in which the coach would point the ball left or right. In groups of four, we had to slide side to side in whatever direction the ball was pointing. It was an extremely hot day, and the Gulf humidity choked the thick air. After about a minute or so of left, right, left, left, etc., Coach Weatherford would then toss the ball into the air. If one of us didn't catch it, we had to start all over again. As the drill dragged on, Coach Weatherford's disposition got hotter and hotter. Eventually, I fell to the ground. I hyperventilated the thick August air to the point where I thought I was going to die. I gasped for every last molecule of oxygen. I had had enough. That was it. This isn't football, I thought. This is just torture. I was done with football. I eventually got myself back together and realized that quitting just wasn't an option. Coach Weatherford wasn't being unfair; that was just his way of teaching.

In my sophomore year I had 41 tackles, four interceptions, and 10 big plays. The next year I tallied 56 tackles, an interception, and 10 more big plays. My senior year brought me 47 tackles, two interceptions, and 11 big plays, and we made it to our first Division I bowl game, earning a 16-14 victory in the Independence Bowl against McNeese State. As a senior, *The Sporting News* named me to the All-South Independent Team and an honorable mention All-American. In addition to the nine picks, I had 188 tackles, 127 of which were solos. We compiled a record of 28-17-1 in my four years.

After my sophomore year, I kept my eye on the NFL Draft. I made note of which defensive backs were drafted, and I compared myself to them. After my sophomore year, I thought that had I been eligible, I probably would have been drafted. After my junior year, I had no doubt I would have gone in the third round or the fourth round. And after my senior year, well, I really believed I would go in the first round.

*   *   *

I was inducted into the M-Club Alumni Association Hall of Fame in 1988 and was named to the school's Football Team of the Century. In 2005, I had the privilege of being inducted into the Mississippi Sports Hall of Fame. Five years later, I became the seventh football player to join the elite USM Legends Club, joining the likes of Reggie Collier, Brett Favre, Ray Guy, Derrick Nix, Sammy Winder, and Fred Cook. Indeed, it is a hell of an honor to be mentioned in the same company with those guys. I took my son to the USM campus, and showed him my former stomping grounds, including the locker room. To this day, it still gets my adrenaline pumping.

"You're on hallowed ground now," I told him.

Some of the bigger games were when we played intrastate teams, such as Mississippi State and Ole Miss. We used to really get up for those games. The crowds were incredible, and we didn't want to let our fans down. It's just a shame those rivalries haven't come back yet. But any time we played a team such as Alabama or Auburn—Southeastern Conference teams with so much talent who always thought they were so much better than we were, and probably should be better—and we took it to them, it was sweet.

Those memories will always stick in my mind, as well as the people who helped me along the way. They all come back to me whenever I get back to Hattiesburg. They were a part of everything I achieved, and I will never forget them and USM. The University doesn't owe me anything. I owe it, and the good and gracious people within it, everything.

CHAPTER FOUR

Drafted Dawg

After my senior season at USM, I was among the top-rated defensive backs coming out of college. I was invited to participate in the 1980 Blue-Gray game and the 1981 Senior Bowl, conveniently played in nearby Mobile. This was going to give me a chance to meet and play in front of coaches from every NFL team. This is where I first met Sam Rutigliano and Marty Schottenheimer. Sam was the head coach for the Browns, and Marty was the defensive coordinator. We chatted and talked, and they intensely watched the workouts. They probably paid more attention to what we were doing in practice than in the game itself.

There was a swirl of speculation in the media of how the Browns might make a deal to improve their draft position. Owner Art Modell, director of player personnel Tommy Prothro, Sam, and head college scout Mike Nixon made it no secret the Browns were openly shopping some key names around to see whether they could move up from the 22nd pick. Greg Pruitt, Johnny Evans, and Thom Darden were likely trade bait, which pleased none of them. Art personally worked the phones trying to see what deal he could cobble together.

Nixon told *The Plain Dealer* this draft was "the weakest in the last five years. It won't be nearly as good as last year's." Wow, only three of the 11 players whom the Browns drafted in 1980 were still with the team a year later. Of the five guys who were drafted in the first two rounds during the previous two drafts, none was a regular. Cleveland Crosby and Sam Claphan, highly touted second-round picks, didn't even make the team. And of the 38 players picked over the previous three years, only 15 were still on roster, and four of them spent most of the time on injured reserve. Three guys drafted the previous year didn't even report to camp, instead defecting to the Canadian Football League. The Browns again had only 11 picks in this draft, with none in rounds two and three. New Orleans had 18 overall. Oakland, the defending Super Bowl champ, had two first-round picks. And this year's crop was going to be worse than last year's? The Browns certainly couldn't afford to make a mistake.

Early in 1981, Browns fans and the organization were still smarting from the icy sting of "Red Right 88." Even the most casual Browns fans have nightmarish flashbacks of that fateful play in the divisional playoff game against the Oakland Raiders in January. Brian Sipe had led the Kardiac Kids down the field through the 30-below-zero wind chill to the Raiders' 13-yard line with 49 seconds remaining and the Browns down, 14-12. Instead of kicking a game-winning field goal, Rutigliano opted for a pass the end zone, not having confidence in struggling veteran kicker Don Cockroft. Sam called Red Right 88 and instructed Brian that if it wasn't wide open, he should throw it to the blonde in the first row of the bleachers (it wasn't the Dawg Pound yet). Brian dropped back and looked for Dave Logan but thought that Ozzie Newsome was a better target. The ball wobbled through the icy air into the hands of defensive back Mike Davis, and the rest is history.

Now, Marty came down to USM to meet with me. We met up at the athletic department and went off to a little restaurant in town. Marty was expecting to ask me the questions, but I turned the tables on him. I asked him the questions. I asked him about the Cleveland Browns organization, the city itself, the defensive scheme, how much man-on-man/bump-and-run defense they did, and how they saw me fitting into their plans.

Marty answered the questions straight on—no dodging or

weaving. It became clear to me that Marty had a brilliant football mind. He knew the game backward and forward, up and down. The Browns definitely had an interest in me, Marty said. I was impressed but had my doubts that I would last until the 22nd pick.

It turned out the Browns had had a similar conversation with Mike Robinson, a speedy defensive end out of Arkansas and from Cleveland's Glenville High School, where he lettered in football, basketball, and track. Mike told *The Cleveland Press* that the Browns said, if I'm "around when they pick, they'd take me" . . . or something like that.

Just before Easter, I got a call from the Browns. They wanted me to come up to their facility at Baldwin-Wallace College in Berea and meet with Sam. On Easter morning, I got on a plane for Cleveland. I was met at the airport by some of the front office personnel, who drove me the short distance to the B-W campus. They led me up the stairs in the Browns' facility, a modest beige-brick building adjacent to B-W's Finnie Stadium, and into Sam's office, just off to the right.

Sam greeted me with his big Italian smile. His wit was in gear, and we enjoyed the light-hearted conversation. As usual, I wanted to do all the talking and ask all the questions, but Sam deftly took control of the interview.

"So, how do you feel about playing in the NFL?" he asked. That was a rather open-ended question, so I took the ball and ran with it.

"It's a dream," I said. "I've been thinking and hoping and planning for this for several years now. I know I have the guts, the strength, the skills. I don't intend on just making the team. I plan to be a starter." If that had been a "real" job interview, those might not have been the best choice of words. But this was the NFL, and confidence, to the point of cockiness, is an attribute, especially for defensive backs.

"We'll definitely keep an eye out for you," Sam said. He didn't promise the Browns would take me if I was still on the board, but I could tell he had great interest.

I went through a bunch of different scenarios in my head. I knew the other top defensive backs available were Ronnie Lott out of Southern California and Kenny Easley out of UCLA. They were both safeties. I figured I was certainly the best cornerback, and I was quite sure I'd go in the first round.

If I could have picked a team to draft me, it would have been the Cowboys. I grew up a Cowboys fan. That would have been the ultimate dream come true. But I knew the Cowboys were drafting 26th, which meant I would have to fall way down in the order, and that meant losing a lot of money.

Even back in 1981, there was a significant drop-off in dollar value the later you were drafted, even in the first round, although not like the multi-million-dollar madness of the modern-day draft. In the past, before there was such a huge dollar difference, some players would tell certain teams not to draft them. Lester Hayes did that in 1977. He told every team not to pick him, except for Dallas and Houston. Hayes, who was from Texas, showed up late to every workout except when scouts from Dallas or Houston were present. The strategy didn't pay off, as he was selected by the Raiders.

I figured the Raiders needed me, the Steelers needed me, and the Browns as well. My guess was that I was going to join Hayes, Al Davis, and the "Just win, baby," gang in Oakland. The *Plain Dealer* held a mock draft, and despite the fact that the Browns were hoping for a running back, their writers predicted the Browns would pick me. *The Cleveland Press* speculated that in the first round I would be picked by San Francisco, while the Browns would pick Mike Robinson.

Nonetheless, the draft has been and always will be a bit of a crapshoot. You can fill a telephone book with the names of guys who by their numbers and physiques should have been sure-fire stars. But for some reason, many just don't have what it takes. Take for example Ron Simmons, a nose tackle who was drafted in the sixth round by the Browns the same year they picked me. Ron was a three-time All-American out of Florida State, twice being first team.

At 240 pounds, with a 20-inch neck, 51-inch chest, 4.6 speed, and the ability to bench-press 525 pounds, he was an amazing physical freak. The papers referred to him as "a potential understudy for the Incredible Hulk." His agent was Jim Smith, the attorney general for the state of Florida. Everyone expected Ron to challenge Henry Bradley for the starting position. Yet Ron couldn't make the team. This is a very physical game, yes, but there is also that mental toughness that you just can't gauge by a guy's blazing 40 time or testosterone-charged bench presses.

A quick, funny story about Henry Bradley: After being cut by the Browns in August 1979, he drove a truck until he got a call to replace the great Jerry Sherk when Jerry came down with a near-fatal staph infection. The following year, the Browns switched to the 3-4 defense, and Henry fit the role of nose tackle beautifully. Always quick and determined, he battled until the final whistle, literally. In 1980, the Browns were looking to clinch the AFC Central title in week 15 in Minnesota. Coming back from a 23-9 deficit, the Vikings' Tommy Kramer flung a Hail Mary pass to Ahmad Rashad as time expired for the winning score. There was no time left on the clock, and the Vikings were up by one. But league rules require that despite the fact that the outcome of the game was not in doubt, an extra point must be attempted unless the score comes in overtime. (This is to accommodate the businessmen in Vegas.) Anyway, most of the Browns had dejectedly left the field when the ref informed Sam he needed to put 11 guys on the field for the extra-point attempt. Henry was one of those 11. Instead of just standing up like the other 10 guys on defense for the pro-forma extra point, Henry rushed in—and blocked the kick.

The Browns have made some great drafts and have blown it in many others. In 1973, the Browns had two picks in each of the first two rounds. Certainly you would think this was a multiple-jackpot scenario. But with those four picks, they chose Steve Holden, Pete Adams, Greg Pruitt, and Jim Stienke. Pruitt turned out to be a great choice; the other three flopped. And the only reason the Browns wound up with Pruitt is because Art, who rarely inserted himself into draft, intervened and told the staff that was the player he wanted. The Browns were very high on Holden, and the Bengals, who drafted just before the Browns, passed on him in favor of Isaac Curtis. The Browns' brain trust celebrated when it heard the news. But Holden went bust, and Curtis spent many fun Sunday afternoons trotting into the end zone with the Browns' secondary feebly lagging behind.

Curtis, by the way, is the reason why the 5-yard chuck rule was instituted. In his rookie year, he was so fast that he often drew double and sometimes triple coverage. The Miami Dolphins took it one step further—they bumped, jammed, dogged, and held him all the way down the field. Other teams followed suit. Paul Brown bitched to the league competition committee, and in 1974, they instituted the "Isaac Curtis Rule." The defender could hit the receiver only once within 5 yards of the line of scrimmage. Anything past that, and it's a 5-yard penalty and an automatic first down.

The media aren't any better when it comes to predicting draft picks' success. One columnist wrote just before the 1957 draft that Jim Brown "doesn't knock anybody down. If the hole wasn't in the line, Brown didn't crack through. If I were a pro scout, I'd drool over Colorado's John Bayuk instead." Good thing the Browns didn't pay much attention to that expert analyst.

And there's the unexpected gold nugget at the bottom of the bucket. Such was the find when the Browns picked Brian Sipe with a 13th-round pick in 1972. Hell, the draft nowadays only goes seven rounds. Brian didn't have all of the great physical tools you look for in a quarterback, but he had all of the intangibles. He rode out the first two seasons on the practice squad, called the "taxi" squad back then. He had the knack of getting the best out of himself and his teammates. He went on to be the chief kid of the Kardiac Kids era.

* * *

The morning of April 28, 1981, I settled in front of the TV with a few other buddies in my apartment in Hattiesburg. With me was teammate Marvin Harvey, a tight end who was also hoping to be drafted. This was the second year ESPN carried the draft live, although it wasn't nearly the glittery Broadway stage show that it is nowadays.

Meanwhile, in Theodore, my parents had a draft party of their own. They invited all of their friends and family to the house, complete with food and drink for the occasion.

Shortly after 10 a.m. Eastern Time, NFL Commissioner Pete Rozelle, looking a little flustered after being stuck in an elevator for 20 minutes, strolled up to the podium, and after dealing with some technical difficulties with the microphone, it was show time.

"With the first pick, the New Orleans Saints select running back George Rogers from South Carolina." No surprise there. Lawrence Taylor, a future Hall of Famer, was taken with the second pick by the Giants, a team for which I worked out (as well as the Steelers and Raiders). Again, no surprise there. I was most interested in seeing where Easley and Lott were going to go. The higher they went, the better it would be for me.

The Jets then took Freeman McNeil. Now on the clock with the fourth pick, the Seahawks took Easley.

"That's great!" I yelled. "Only the fourth pick and Easley's already off the board." That was like taking the $1 case within your first set of picks on *Deal or No Deal*. I could hear the ringing of cash registers in the back of my head. Now I wanted to see Lott get picked.

The Packers were next, and they took quarterback Rich Campbell. Then Tampa Bay took Hugh Green. This was getting nerve-wracking. I didn't know what to think. Next came San Francisco with the eighth pick.

"The San Francisco 49ers select Ronnie Lott out of the University of Southern California."

Now I was feeling good. We weren't even one third of the way through the first round, and Lott and Easley were gone. I figured I would certainly be the next defensive back to be picked. The Rams needed some defensive help, and they were next. They took Mel Owens, a linebacker out of Michigan.

OK, I figured. Any moment now. I sat on the edge of my seat every time Rozelle sauntered back to the podium. The Bengals then took David Verser out of Kansas.

OK, I thought, they needed some offensive help. For sure, my time was coming soon. Very soon. But the Bears, Colts, Dolphins, and Chiefs then all decided they needed offensive help, too.

Damn! We were now up to the 15th pick. Surely someone needed a top-notch, speedy, loud-mouthed, cocky shutdown corner. And yes, the Broncos indeed needed a corner. So they picked Dennis Smith from USC.

Dammit! I'm better than him! What the hell was going on? I got up and paced the room like an expectant father.

Pick 16 was Detroit's. Mark Nichols, a wide receiver from San Jose State. This was getting serious.

Now came the Steelers. I know they were looking for defensive help. They had scouted me, and at least at one point were considering picking me if I were available, but one of their scouting staff referred to me, supposedly in jest, as a "midget." It turns out that the scout was actually using a writer from *Pro Football Weekly* to throw everyone off the trail, and that, indeed, the Steelers had significant interest in me. So when Rozelle came to the podium with that card, I thought that was going to be the moment. I liked the idea of going to a team that had four Super Bowl rings and was a top playoff contender, year in and year out. I could fit into their scheme well. This was going to be it.

"With the 17th pick, the Pittsburgh Steelers select . . . Keith Gary, defensive end, Oklahoma."

Ah, fuck 'em. So they think I'm a midget? I decided right there that whenever I met the Steelers on the field, there was going to be hell to pay. Punishment. Who wants to play for those damn inbred hillbillies, anyway?

All right, now the Baltimore Colts were up. Down went defensive tackle Donnell Thompson from North Carolina. Down one more step I went.

Next came the Patriots. No sale. They took tackle Brian Holloway out of Stanford. Another lineman went next, Mark May of Pitt, to the Washington Redskins.

That meant we were at pick number 21. And the Oakland Raiders were up. Now, this had to be it. They were looking for a defensive back, I was clearly the best one up. I had figured I would be going to them anyway, so I sat next to the phone, waiting for what was sure to be a congratulatory call from Al Davis, who had personally told me that if I were still available when their pick came up, they'd take me.

"With the 21st pick, the Oakland Raiders select . . . Ted Watts, defensive back, Texas Tech."

I bolted out of the chair. "What the hell . . . !" I yelled. Ted Watts? Those Raiders had to be out of their fucking minds. Ted Watts? This had to be a joke. Shit! I stewed around the apartment, muttering to myself, wondering what the hell had gone wrong. How could I have fallen this far? And just what the hell did the Raiders see in Ted Watts? I sat down again and saw that the Browns were now up. I was still pissed at the Raiders. I didn't notice that the time on the clock was running down on the Browns. This ordeal had now dragged out for three agonizing hours.

Then the phone rang. I answered.

"Hello, this is Art Modell. Is this Hanford Dixon?"

"Uh, yes sir, Mr. Modell. This is Hanford Dixon." I was awestruck. This was one of the great owners of the NFL, and he was now on the phone with me. I froze in anticipation of what he was about to say next.

"Well, Hanford," he said in that beautiful Brooklyn accent, "how would you like to play for the Cleveland Browns?"

I could barely utter a word. It was happening. I was about to be drafted by one of the great franchises of the NFL. "Uh, yes, certainly, Mr. Modell. It would be an honor."

"Well, good then," Art said. "We're about to draft you."

"That's great, Mr. Modell. Thank you ever so much. I can't wait to get there to Cleveland."

I hung up the phone, and we all let out a hoot and holler. We jumped around and danced, but I wanted to act cool. Just a few months earlier, I had sat in my living room and watched the Browns lose to the Raiders on the infamous Red Right 88 call. I saw those crazy, nutty fans, some running around shirtless in the 4-degree weather, and figured no way would I want to get mixed up with that shit. But now I was the first-round pick of the Cleveland Browns! I knew the first call I had to make was to my parents. I dialed the phone, and just as my mother answered, Pete Rozelle made his way to the podium, with just 56 seconds left on the Browns' clock.

"Momma!" I yelled.

Meanwhile, Rozelle began to read the card.

"With the 22nd pick . . . " Rozelle started into his cadence.

"Momma!" I yelled again.

" . . . The Cleveland Browns select . . ."

"Oh baby, I know, I know, I know, I know!"

" . . . Hanford Dixon, defensive back, University of Southern Mississippi."

My mother could hardly contain herself. She was thrilled beyond belief. Then I talked a few minutes with my dad; he, too, was relishing the moment. I talked to my sister as well as my uncle. We hung up the phone, then it began ringing nonstop. I was now a media figure.

Meanwhile, Mike Robinson decided he needed to go for a long walk. But good news for him was still to come.

While I was delighted to be drafted in the first round by the Browns, I was still ticked off that I hadn't gone sooner. I was determined to show all 21 teams who had passed on me that they were wrong, especially Pittsburgh and Oakland.

Two rounds later, we celebrated again as Marvin was picked in the third round by Kansas City. He didn't have much of a career, appearing in only seven games. As for Watts, he played four years with the Raiders, one with the Giants, and one with the Chargers. He had a total of five interceptions in his career, something that I did in one season—twice. Others who were picked after me include Marion Barber, Neil Lomax, Cris Collinsworth, and future Hall of Famers Rickey Jackson, Mike Singletary, Howie Long, and Russ Grimm.

The Browns didn't get their running back. Sam later said that the only runners they would have chosen over me had they still been available would have been Rogers or McNeil, and both of them were gone by the third pick. The Browns didn't draft again until the fourth round, picking up Mike Robinson, fulfilling his dream of being drafted by his hometown team. They also selected Steve Cox, a great kicker, nose tackle Ron Simmons, linebacker Eddie Johnson, guard Randy Schleusener, defensive end Dean Prater, defensive back Larry Friday, and offensive lineman Kevin McGill. Out of the crew, only I, Eddie, Mike, and Steve made the regular squad—Larry and Kevin were put on injured reserve.

Dad put up a big Browns sign in front of the house. All of his work buddies congratulated him. Mom was thrilled beyond belief. She and Debra never missed a Browns home game until Mom was just too sick to travel. Even while in the hospital, Mom would have my games on TV, and would proudly say to anyone and everyone, "There's Number 29. That's my baby! Look at him go!"

Reporters from all over the country wanted to talk to me. I took the time to talk to them all. In an attempt to get things off on the right foot with the Cleveland fans, I temporarily forgot that the Cowboys had been my favorite NFL team through the years. While talking with Russell Schneider of *The Plain Dealer*, I fudged a little bit and said that the Browns had been my favorite team for a long time. Well, if you consider a couple hours to be a long time, I was telling the truth.

All of this good news did lead to one of the biggest mistakes of my life. Now that I was headed to the NFL and was about to sign a big, fat contract with a hefty signing bonus, I blew off my last semester of school. I didn't get my degree, a huge regret I have to this day. But I am going to remedy that. Come hell or high water, I will finally finish that degree. Dick Schafrath returned to Ohio State as a full-time student 50 years after he was drafted by the Browns. In 2006, Dick, at age 69, got his degree. Trust me, it won't take me that long.

CHAPTER FIVE

Cleveland Dawg

I put on my best white suit, with matching white shoes, and looked slick and sharp. I boarded a plane to Cleveland. Upon arrival at Hopkins Airport, the media were there with cameras and microphones at the ready. And there I was, in my all-white getup. I was the top dog in the house. We went over to the Middleburg Heights Holiday Inn, where the Cleveland Touchdown Club was hosting a reception. There I met Ozzie Newsome and Ricky Feacher, two other good ol' southern boys like me. Ozzie had been called by Bear Bryant "the finest receiver in the history of Alabama."

I walked into the room, and they began to point and laugh.

"What the hell is a southern country boy like you doing wearing that shit?" Ozzie laughed. Greg Pruitt and Ron Bolton also got in some jabs.

Their catcalls and mocking barbs didn't register with me. I strolled around like the top dog I was. I was a first-round NFL Draft pick, and that entitled me to wear a white suit if I fucking felt like it. Besides, we were going to have some workouts over the next few days, and I'd prove myself there. I was going to play like a number-one pick. But still, I realized I was in the company of the best. While being cocky, yes, I still was grateful for the chance to play in the NFL. So at first, it was yes, Mr. Pruitt. Yes, Mr. Sipe. Yes, Mr. Newsome.

But minicamp showed me I wasn't as good as I thought I was. I was among nine draftees and 19 free agents who reported to camp May 3. Everyone reported on time except for Mike Robinson, who, ironically, lived in Cleveland.

We started with physical exams over at the Cleveland Clinic, where a couple of guys got rejected because of bad knees, and began two-a-day open workouts at George Finnie Stadium on the campus of Baldwin-Wallace College, where the Browns' headquarters were located. I was assigned number 40, a number chosen at random. I would have liked to have continued to wear 19, but league rules prohibited that number for a defensive back. Later, I got to choose my number, and that's when I selected 29, figuring I'd keep the 9 and just change the first digit by one.

I was big shit for college ball, yes, but this was now the NFL. In college, each team had a few guys who were bigger and faster than the rest. But in the NFL, everyone was not just big and fast, but world class. I quickly realized that the transition from college to pro was exponentially more difficult than that from high school to college.

I've been asked if it's harder nowadays for college players to make it into the NFL. It's very hard, yes, but not necessarily harder. One has to prepare, prepare, prepare, both physically and mentally. That won't ever change.

*   *   *

During minicamp, there had to be some drama and posturing for negotiating purposes. Two days into minicamp, both Mike Robinson and Ron Simmons walked out. I'm sure their agents told them to do so. And I can see their point. The free agents had to sign their contracts before participating. We draftees still were unsigned, participating in a non-required event. Had someone blown out a knee or suffered some freak injury, his value would tank. In fact, I bruised my knee during one of the sessions. Not a big deal, but I could see how it could have become one. But Ron and Mike came back later that day, clearly wanting to prove their worth.

I was among eight players who were asked to stay for the three-day veterans' minicamp that followed ours. In that camp I had to cover Ricky Feacher, Reggie Rucker, Dave Logan, and Willis Adams. Damn, they were fast!

They all brought their special talents to the field. Logan was a big, tall dude who maybe wasn't as fast as others but could always get open. He had the biggest hands I'd ever seen. He could have caught a watermelon catapulted 200 yards at him. Even though he was near the end of his career, Reggie still had great hands, ran great routes, and knew how to set you up, especially if you were a young guy. And Willis was just plain fast.

I took some lumps, getting beaten on some short and long routes. Just a couple of weeks prior, I had worked out for the New York Giants, and I pulled my hamstring pretty badly. It was better, but still I got turned around a few times and got beaten deep a couple of times in both the one-on-one and the seven-on-seven drills.

In this league, you have to have a short memory. You have to believe that you belong at this level or you'll get run out in a hurry, especially in the position I played. If you make a mistake at defensive back, everybody sees it, and all too often, your opponent is prancing down the sideline with the ball. You have to be prepared mentally and physically seven days a week, as well as on every down. The guys on the other side of the ball are looking for your weaknesses. Opposing coaches pore over film for hours looking for your vulnerabilities and potential mismatches. If you have a weakness, they'll find it. They all take it very seriously—as a business—because it is a business.

I made my fair share of errors in minicamp, but my speed allowed me to compensate and close whatever gaps the receivers could stretch out. Covering those guys allowed me to get a good feel for the different varieties, styles, and techniques receivers had at this level. It was a tough camp, but I thought that, all in all, I performed well, and that the coaches and staff saw I had the ability. Jed Hughes was the defensive backs coach, and he pointed out some of the things I had to learn.

Sheer athleticism goes a long way, but you have to have more than that, especially at defensive back. Technique takes you to the next level. Head position is a good example. If a receiver runs an out on me, I'm going to run the route with him, but I'm not going to look at the quarterback unless I'm close enough to touch the receiver. If all my attention is on him so that my head position focuses me on the receiver and I get close enough to touch him, then I look back at the quarterback. Often, I would be in perfect position to intercept the ball or at least knock it away. Now, if he tries to double-move me, I wouldn't lose sight of him. Head position and hand position are critical. You always have to keep your body low. That allows you to move and shift without any false steps. When you're going up against the fastest guys in the world and they know where they're going and you don't, you've got some serious problems if you don't have top technique.

*   *   *

In early July I finally signed my first contract with the Browns. I got a series of three one-year deals, with an option for a fourth year. My first-year salary was $80,000. Nowadays, the rookie minimum is $390,000. I got a bonus check for $150,000—until Walter Payton got his damn hands on it (more about that later). My agent, Bud Holmes, who was also Walter's agent, did a great job putting together the deal. It turned out to be better than I had expected. Bud got me a good mix of guarantees and incentives. I asked my mother if she needed anything, and she assured me, no, she was fine. I still bought her a new white Buick Park Avenue. I bought myself a white Jeep Cherokee and drove it with the top down from Hattiesburg to Cleveland. That was a rough ride.

My good friend Ozzie Newsome is now the general manager of

the Baltimore Ravens. He told me that he just offered a rookie $4 million, and that rookie told Ozzie he was "insulted." Hell, I wish I could have been insulted like that. Four million is an insult? *Sheeit.*

I rented an apartment in what was then known as Park Centre in downtown Cleveland. A year later, I bought a condo on the eighth floor of the Lake House on Edgewater Drive in Lakewood. I purchased the unit from a company called Professional Investments of America, whose president was Howard Ferguson, the coach who established wrestling dynasty at St. Edward High in Lakewood.

*   *   *

I was headed to the 36th training camp in Browns history. The original Browns, founded in 1946 by taxicab entrepreneur Arthur B. "Mickey" McBride, held their camp on the campus of Bowling Green State University. At that camp, history was quietly made when Bill Willis and Marion Motley were brought in for a try-out. These men not only made the team but went on to the Hall of Fame—while breaking the color barrier in football. Coach Paul Brown ran a tight ship—there was no smoking in the locker room or dining hall, ties and jackets to be worn in public, weekly tests, and an 11 p.m. curfew. And during the season, players were told not to have sex after Tuesdays. Now how that one could have been enforced, I have no idea.

In order to be a bit closer to Cleveland, camp was moved to Hiram, Ohio, on the hilly campus of Hiram College six years later. That brought more fan interest during the training season. Those were the golden years of training camp for the Browns, who had only two losing seasons during their 23-year stay there. The club was housed in a women's dorm. Someone discovered a nudist camp nearby. Many players then skipped post-practice trips and headed to a bar in nearby Garrettsville to play some volleyball.

With the expansion of the roster, and because of the lack of air conditioning in the Hiram dorms and the need for more practice space, camp was moved to the campus of Kent State University in 1975. It was moved to Lakeland Community College in 1982 and eventually to the new Cleveland Browns' year-round facility in Berea.

On July 17, 1981, I reported to training camp on the campus of Kent State University, about an hour's drive southeast of Cleveland. We stayed at Beall Hall, where I roomed with Lawrence Johnson, the veteran cornerback whose starting position I openly coveted. I was one of 40 rookies and free agents, all of whom started camp a week before the veterans were to arrive. However, a handful of veterans showed up early because they had something to prove or they just wanted to make sure no rookies were getting any crazy ideas of taking their positions.

We ran through the standard 90-minute two-a-day practices in the often-scorching July sun. The first practice was at 8:45 a.m. The second one began at 3:30 p.m. One thing I noticed right away was the large turnout of fans for the workouts and practices, which were held at KSU's Dix Stadium. During camp, the rookies were paid $300 per week; the veterans got $500 per week.

One of the things the rookies had to do was put on a show for the veterans. Some guys sang, danced, told jokes, or played an instrument. I gave singing a try but was booed off the stage.

The Browns started me out at left cornerback, which might have been more of a negotiating strategy with Ron Bolton. Ron was the starting left cornerback, and he got the Browns going in the Red Right 88 game by picking off a Jim Plunkett pass and speed skating 42 yards across the frozen stadium tundra for a touchdown for the game's first score. But the Browns and Ron were in a rather intense negotiation on his contract, and by me working out at his position during rookie week, I'm sure the Browns were sending him a message, despite his admirable six interceptions in 1980 and 33 over his career.

In the rookie scrimmage against Buffalo the first weekend of camp I got some work in at left corner despite bruising my knee the day before. Nonetheless, Ron did report to camp, and I was switched over to the right corner position, where I was going to compete with Lawrence, a third-year pro out of Wisconsin, where he was a Big Ten sprint champion. The Browns picked him up in the second round of the 1979 draft. Lawrence and I were alike in many ways. We were both quick, aggressive, and had great closing speed. He was a little bit bigger than I was; I was a trifle faster than he was. Despite the fact that he was a veteran and I was a loud-mouthed, cocky rookie who wanted to take his job, Lawrence was very helpful and took the time to explain things to me. I learned a lot from him, not just from what he said but from watching his technique. He had an exceptional ability to turn tightly while running. I noticed how he never rounded off his turns while covering a receiver. He showed no ill effects from the fractured shoulder he had suffered in the season's home opener the year before. Despite competing with each other, we got along exceptionally well, mainly because we both knew what we were there for—to win a Super Bowl. I made myself better pushing Lawrence for the starting spot, and he got better trying to keep me and my rookie ass in place.

In the scrimmage against Buffalo, played in Edinboro, Pennsylvania, in front of about 6,500 people, I played well. I made a couple of big hits and knocked down some passes. But, like I said earlier, you have to be ready on every down, and on one play, the Bills' Larry Taylor got between me and Larry Friday to catch a 27-yard pass. Coach Sam gave passing grades to me and to Mike Robinson and Ron Simmons. Veteran cornerback Ron Bolton and safety Thom Darden gave me the nickname "Super Rook."

*   *   *

The next week opened the exhibition season, which featured the Browns playing the Falcons in the Hall of Fame Game in Canton. But in what would become a prophetic mishap, I pulled a groin muscle during practice that week and viewed the game from the

sideline. But the following week was going to be the real test. The
goddamn Steelers were coming to town. It may have only been an
exhibition game, but I was determined to show those jokers just
what a midget could do to them.

Nearly 80,000 people showed up at the old stadium for this
game. While the Hall of Fame Game against the Falcons the week
before was a de facto home game for us, only some 21,000 people
filled Fawcett Stadium. They made a lot of noise, but shit, these
78,000 nutty fans were just crazy—and it was just a damn exhibition game. I noticed the difference inside the pre-Cambrian-era
locker room, too. Even the veterans were snapping the chin straps
a little tighter than you would expect for an exhibition game.

It was my baptism into one of the fiercest rivalries in all of sports.

I blocked an extra point in the first quarter, but the goddamn
Steelers got to kick it again because of a penalty. In the second
quarter, I was given my chance. The goddamn Steelers still had
their starting receivers in the game, so I got my first live game action against the likes of Lynn Swann and John Stallworth (who was
recovering from a foot injury).

For some reason, our pass rush was ineffective, and Cliff Stoudt,
an Ohio boy (Oberlin High School and Youngstown State), made
the most of it. But I hung with Swann and Stallworth fairly well—
until I violated my own rule on technique. With about a minute and
a half to go in the second quarter, Swann lined up on the right side,
and I was opposite him at left corner. I had been instructed that if
Swann lines up tight, he's going to the outside. So when he took a
step inside, I didn't step inside with him. I looked at Stoudt before
I could get a hand on Swann, so when I looked back for Swann, he
was gone—with the football—for a 25-yard score. Damn, he was
so fast. Then just as the first half ended, Stallworth beat me to the
ball in the end zone for a 5-yard touchdown. Damn it again. In my
first 93 seconds of professional football, I already had been beaten
twice for touchdowns.

Then I remembered the very wise words of my mother: Put God

first in your life, and everything else will come together. I reminded myself of that truth, and that I did indeed belong in this league at this place and time.

I got my head and act together in the third quarter, picking off Stoudt for my first interception. We lost, 35-31, but despite my getting beaten for those two scores, Coach Sam actually had some nice words for me in the morning paper.

"I was pleased with a lot of things Dixon did," he told *The Plain Dealer*. A few days later, Sam hinted that I might actually challenge for a starting role. Even Ron Bolton, whom I replaced in the second quarter, said some nice things. He told *The Plain Dealer*, "He is a great athlete and has a lot of natural ability. I can see why he was a number-one pick. I also like Dixon's style. He is aggressive and cocky, which all good defensive backs must be. He reminds me of myself." Ron did wind up getting that new contract through 1984 that he had sought just before the regular season began.

We lost to Buffalo, 31-20, in an exhibition game. I did OK again but got beaten by Byron Franklin in a horrible fourth quarter.

*   *   *

Meanwhile, the main drama of camp didn't involve me. It was the battle between Don Cockroft and Dave Jacobs for the kicking position. Drafted out of Adams State in Colorado in the third round in 1967, Don in 1968 replaced the legendary Lou Groza, who had been with the Browns since 1946. Don was one of the last straight-on place kickers in the league. Now 36, he wasn't necessarily old for a kicker, but he was coming off knee surgery and a herniated disk, and had struggled in the past few years. He missed field goals of 47 and 30 yards and an extra point in the Red Right 88 debacle the previous January. Two days later, Don, whose field-goal percentage was tops in the NFL from 1968 to 1979, picked up the morning paper and found out that the Browns had signed Dave Jacobs.

Don's kickoffs now rarely reached the goal line, often coming down around the 10 and being returned close to the 30. Coach Sam told reporters that Don needed "to get his act together." But Don wasn't ready to retire, and he was as determined as ever to retain his spot. He underwent surgery on his left knee January 22, correcting not only his knee but issues with his back and sciatic nerve. You have to admire his determination and character.

Don is one of the nicest guys you'll ever meet, and a devout Christian. He even spoke at a Billy Graham crusade at the old stadium in 1972. You couldn't help but root for him, but this is a business.

Neither Dave nor Don had impressive exhibition seasons, and in the last exhibition game against the Packers, the kickers missed three extra points between the two of them. Don missed two, and slowly walked off the field, and it was pretty obvious he was doing the slow walk to the gallows. You just knew those were his last steps. The next evening, Don was at the dinner table with his wife and kids. His wife offered up the dinner blessing and asked God to give Coach Sam great wisdom in making the difficult decision in front of him. Three minutes later, the phone rang, and Sam answered the prayer, but not in the way Don and his family had hoped.

Dave didn't know he had won the job—becoming only the fourth kicker in Browns history—until reporters contacted him. But Dave turned out to be a flop. A huge flop. Although he was the all-time leading scorer for Syracuse University, had a black belt in tae kwon do, and had once kicked a 76-yard field goal in practice, he was cut by Denver, New England, and the Jets—twice. That should have provided some clues as to what was coming next. Don told Sam that Dave was a flaky kicker, and he turned out to be right. Against Houston at the Stadium in the second game of the regular season, Dave missed three field goals. Two of them were low-trajectory kicks that were blocked by 35-year-old Elvin Bethea, who said after the game, "Those were for Cockroft. Us old-timers have to stick together."

Dave went on to go 4-for-12 before he and his ballerina-like size

7 shoe were given the boot. The Browns traded a ninth-round pick to San Francisco for Matt Bahr, who turned out to be a steal.

*   *   *

During cut-down, many guys were on edge. Nervous players would constantly review their mental depth charts, examining all possible scenarios. A couple of guys, sometimes assistant coaches, sometimes front office people, were know as "turks." They delivered the bad news. You got a knock on the door, and one of the turks would say, "Coach wants to see you. And bring your playbook."

Some guys just took it in stride, appreciative of having the opportunity to give pro football a try. Others just went freakin' nuts. You could hear the yelling and screaming through the halls, with furniture crashing against the walls. Most of the guys who didn't react well claimed they never got the chance to demonstrate what they had. They might have felt that way, but in this business, you need to produce big at the outset. No more time for development. This was the big show.

I never feared the turks. Even the sportswriters were saying that not only was I a shoo-in, but I would compete for the starting job.

I'm sure it must have been difficult for Sam to let the air out of so many men's dreams. He did so frankly and honestly. Same thing for Marty when he was head coach. As a player, Marty himself got cut twice in his six-year career. I can't imagine sitting across a desk and looking at someone like Curtis Weathers, Johnny Davis, Dick Ambrose, or Robert Jackson and telling them that they were through. But every few days, usually after breakfast, you'd find a group of long-faced, large men waiting silently among an array of suitcases at the entrance to Beall Hall for the van that must have looked more like a hearse, and that whisked them away to the airport. The club picked up the airfare.

Another grizzly veteran who got a visit from the turk was linebacker Charlie Hall. He had started 104 games at outside linebacker dating back to 1971. But with the 3-4 defense, we needed linebackers with speed, and Charlie had lost a bit, just as any 32-year-old would after 10 years in the league. Charlie was a tough as they come and a helluva great guy as well. Although I was just a rookie, I realized the value his character and leadership were to this team. It was sad to see him go. He was offered a deal by the Baltimore Colts but turned it down, returning to his ranch in Yoakum, Texas.

Meanwhile, Jerry Sherk was on the comeback trail. Jerry was a four-time Pro Bowl defensive tackle but was trying to overcome the effects of two knee operations.

In the early to mid-1970s Jerry teamed up with the great Walter Johnson, giving the Browns arguably the best defensive tackle tandem in the league. Both guys were big, strong, and quick as cats. One time, Jerry got knocked on his ass but bounced up and made the tackle 40 yards downfield.

Jerry was known for his contrasting performances in two Monday night games. The first one, against the Jets in 1970, the first *Monday Night Football* game ever, the Jets picked on Jerry. He took it on the chin from both Howard Cosell and the Jets—the former ranted about the slightest misstep and went so far as to blame Jerry for a play that ran the other way; the latter gave him eight stitches. But in 1979, in a Monday nighter against the Cowboys, Jerry had a helluva game, sacking Roger Staubach 3½ times, and Cosell then recanted: "He's one of the best in the league, and he has been for a decade."

Jerry scraped open a boil on his elbow on the Astroturf in Philadelphia later that year, and a staph infection set in. It settled in his left knee. He could have lost his leg or even his life. He spent five weeks at the Cleveland Clinic battling the infection and the allergic reaction to the antibiotic he was given to treat it. But Jerry fought through it all. He lost 35 pounds through the ordeal but had put it back on and at age 33 was determined to play. And the Browns needed him. In the Kardiac Kids year of 1980, most of which Jerry missed, the Browns were last in the NFL in pass defense and 23rd overall.

Things didn't look so good for Jerry a few months before camp, as his knee kept hurting and was swelling after workouts. But he then was treated for a sinus infection, and apparently the anti-inflammatory nature of the sinus medicine also relieved the inflammation and pain in his knee.

Jerry came to camp figuring he would give it nine days to see whether his knee could hold up. It did, and so did he. A week before minicamp back in May, Jerry was about to announce his retirement. He made the team but saw only limited action, mostly when we used four down linemen on passing situations. Jerry was quite the shutterbug—always taking pictures. Actually, he's a pretty damn good photographer. And he's also a damn good guy. After his retirement from football, he got an advanced degree in psychology and now works with at-risk kids.

Another preseason drama involved Thom Darden and Clinton Burrell. Thom unquestionably was the greatest safety the Browns ever had, collecting 45 interceptions over his career. He also was ranked fourth among the NFL's hardest hitters by *Sport* magazine. He often was given license to freelance his coverages to wherever he saw the best chance to snare an errant pass. But at age 30, the former Sandusky High School and University of Michigan star was beginning to slow a bit, and this is a speed game.

The second week into camp, the coaching staff broke the news to Thom that they were going to give Clinton a shot at free safety. Clinton was fast and tough, and Sam figured he would be a better starter. That incensed Thom, who demanded that he either be the starter or be traded. The Browns did neither, but after the second week of the season, Clinton went down with a knee injury and Thom resumed his role as the leader of the secondary.

*   *   *

The regular season was now upon us. Two of *The Plain Dealer's* three big writers, Russell Schneider and Hal Lebovitz, picked us to win the division. Chuck Heaton picked the Steelers. *The Cleveland*

Press also picked us to win the division. A survey by the Pro Football Writers Association predicted the San Diego Chargers would win the AFC title, with the Browns second. And our first game of the year was against those Chargers, on Monday night.

The Chargers were led by quarterback Dan Fouts and their high-powered "Air Coryell" offense. Gib Shanley, the great radio play-by-play voice of the Browns from 1961 to 1984, summed it up by saying, "The last team with the ball will win."

We were still sporting the "Kardiac Kids" moniker; however, we weren't kids anymore. In fact, with an average age on our club at 26.7 years, only six teams in the league were older. By the end of the season, the "Kardiac Kids" name had pretty much faded away.

It was a beautiful September evening, and the whole hype and show of *Monday Night Football* was on display for my first regular-season game. Lawrence was the starter at right corner, but I looked forward to getting some licks in covering kickoffs. All the splendor and glory of the NFL and the extra splash that was *Monday Night Football* were now before me. Talk about a kid at Christmas!

The 79,000-plus fans roared with the opening kick, but by halftime, they were booing. Fouts had his way with our defense, in one stretch completing 15 consecutive passes, two short of the NFL record, and finished the night with 330 yards in the air. We were blasted, 44-14, as the Chargers racked up 535 yards. I watched Lawrence take on 13-year veteran Charlie Joiner throughout the game, and it was pretty tough to watch. Despite his speed and toughness, Lawrence got turned around and beaten several times.

Brian Sipe had a helluva game, but his 31 completions in 57 attempts—both club records—could muster only 14 points.

The next week, our defense improved considerably, holding Ken Stabler and Earl Campbell in check, but the offense took the day off as we lost to Houston, 9-3. Fans and media now worried openly about which direction the season was headed. Decisions and changes had to be made. It was now my time.

Lawrence's knee was bothering him, so Marty Schottenheimer

told me that I was going to get the start. It was pretty much kept quiet—the sportswriters didn't know the decision had been made until I took the field as a starter for the first time on September 20, 1981, in Cincinnati. My moment had arrived. All that hard work was paying off. I was now going to be a starter in the NFL. I was determined that this was not a one-shot deal. I was going to be the permanent starter.

There was plenty of bad blood between us and the Bengals. They were coached by Forrest Gregg, who had quit the Browns in a very bitter separation in 1977 after realizing he was going to be fired. In December 1980, Thom absolutely laid out Bengals wide receiver/punter Pat McInally with a forearm shot to the neck, drawing a $1,000 fine. Tacked on the bulletin board in the Bengals' locker room was a picture of Thom with a made-up quote penciled that read, "Give me another shot at the skinny, guitar-playing intellectual." (McInally was a Harvard graduate). Also, linebacker Robert Jackson supposedly spat into Bengals running back Archie Griffin's face several times. Word was that the Bengals had a contract out on Robert. We signed kick returner Cleotha Montgomery to replace the injured Dino Hall, and Cleotha wanted to break one against the team that had cut him three weeks earlier. He told us to be careful. Add to that the fact that several of our key guys were hurt, and the potential for a real donnybrook existed.

I couldn't wait to get in there. I was going to take on McInally, Isaac Curtis, and rookie Cris Collinsworth. I was also going to have to chase the two great Ohio State backs—Griffin and Pete Johnson. Johnson was a big, tough, punishing runner. Secretly, I didn't look forward to tangling with him. But as the game progressed and I got some good hits in, I realized I had nothing to fear.

It was a great first half for us as our offense maintained great ball control. We held the ball for half of the first quarter on our opening drive, and then another 13-play drive. Despite moving the ball well, we had to settle for two field goals. After Eddie Johnson made a touchdown-saving tackle on the kickoff after the second field goal, our O continued its dominance, going 80 yards in eight plays. Brian Sipe hit Reggie Rucker for a 49-yard pass and then found Ozzie Newsome for a 4-yard score.

Keeping the opposing offense off the field is indeed the best defense, and we just shut them down. The Bengals couldn't pick up a single first down in the first quarter. They got it in gear a bit in the second quarter and were lined up for a field goal just before the half. But I swooped in and blocked it as the half expired.

Bengals quarterback Ken Anderson tried to pick on me in the second half, thinking that since I was a rookie I would be a weak link. We were up, 13-3, going into the fourth quarter. Collinsworth got loose for a 41-yard score on a play where I gambled and tried to jump the pattern but failed to come up with the ball. Then Mike Pruitt retaliated with a 12-yard TD run.

But the big play came late in the fourth as the Bengals were trying to make a comeback. Anderson let fly a deep throw for Isaac Curtis. I played him and the ball perfectly, and the pass fell incomplete. But sitting there on the carpet was a penalty flag. Interference? On me? It was a shitty call, but I guess that since my back was to the ball, the ref thought otherwise. I had to quickly get it out of my head and just play on. That gave the Bengals the ball at the 1, and three plays later, Johnson rammed it in to close it to 20-17.

With a bit over two minutes left and all three timeouts still unused, the Bengals decided to forego the onside kick. But our offense came through again and ran out the clock, with Brian hitting Reggie on a 13-yard pass and juggling catch that gave us a critical first down. Our offense controlled the ball that day for nearly 42 minutes. That made our job on defense quite a bit easier. We should have had two more touchdowns, too, as Ozzie committed a rare drop of a sure TD and Brian got called for an odd motion penalty.

It turns out that the anticipated retaliations against Robert and Thom never happened. In fact, before the game Thom and McInally met at midfield and shook hands. Robert did get in Griffin's face a couple of times, but Griffin didn't say anything much.

The next morning, Lebovitz wrote in his column that I "could be the defensive back the Browns long have been seeking." No doubt, Hal. But not everyone was impressed. Schneider wrote in his column that "the killer instinct" was missing in the Browns.

But I was now the starter and would remain a starter for the rest of my career. The previous year's number-one pick, Charles White, also secured his role as a starter, replacing Greg Pruitt, who would eventually be traded to Oakland.

*   *   *

The next week we cruised by the previously undefeated Falcons at home, and it appeared we were firing on all cylinders once again. Our defense was seventh in the AFC and our offense had climbed to third. But we went on to lose nine of our last 12, and finished in the basement of the AFC Central with a sucky 5-11 record. I finished the year with 47 tackles, 29 of them solo, and was fortunate to be named to the All-Rookie Team.

Although I was all of 170 pounds, I looked forward to taking shots at the big boys, like Pete Johnson and later Earl Campbell. By December of my rookie year, the Browns were mired in last place, but I looked forward to taking on Campbell when we went to Houston for a nationally televised Thursday night game on December 3.

"Damn. You haven't seen Earl Campbell," my teammates told me all week.

"Well, Earl Campbell hasn't seen Hanford Dixon," I responded with all due cockiness.

Early in the game, Campbell came around the left side on a sweep. I fixed my eyes on him and charged forward. He looked at me and took aim, and *bam!* I saw stars. It was just like running into that telephone pole while playing football with my friends back in Theodore. The first thing I thought to myself was, "Oh shit. I'm hurt." But I wasn't about to let Campbell, or any of the Oilers for that matter, see me hurt. It's not just a pride thing. If the opposing coaches upstairs see that you're hurt, they'll run a go pattern past your sagging ass on the next play. So I jumped up, maintained my composure as best I could, jogged to the sideline, and sat my ass down. After a second or two, I realized something was wrong. I was sitting on the wrong bench, on the wrong sideline. I jumped up and trotted over to our sideline, much to the amusement of the veterans. We went on to lose that game, 17-13.

*   *   *

As a rookie I had my duties for the veterans. We rookies got them drinks, ran errands for them, carried bags, brought doughnuts, pretty much the same type of stuff pledges do at fraternities. We got our share of perks, too, one of which got me the wrath of Lyle Alzado.

Lyle was an unpredictable soul. Some days, he came to practice and was the nicest guy you'd ever met. Other times, he was just plain crazy nuts. You never knew which Lyle was going to show up each day. His use of steroids is well documented, and it may have been messing with his head.

Some of us were given tickets to a show at the Front Row Theater. I went to the show, and as I took my seat, I saw Lyle sitting a few rows back. I smiled and said hi, but instead of responding in kind, Lyle's eyes began to bulge. He did a slow seethe, and at first I couldn't figure out what I had said or done. I was getting worried because I knew that when Lyle exploded, there was nothing that could contain him. This was a guy who held his own in an exhibition boxing match with Muhammad Ali. Lyle's eyes fixed on me. He slowly rose to his feet, and I heard him mutter, "How the hell . . . ?" Then I realized what was going on. Lyle was pissed to no end that I, a rookie, had a better seat than he did. I certainly knew better than to fuck with him, especially in a public theater. I just quietly turned around and sank my ass into my seat, which thankfully defused the situation.

But in November, I fell victim to the turkey trick. As a rookie, I had to run errands or pick things up for the veterans. So just before

Thanksgiving, there was a notice on the bulletin board that anyone who wanted a free turnkey could sign up for one. Of course, most everyone's name was on that list. So Mike Robinson and I were designated to go pick up all these turkeys at some turkey farm in central Ohio. Now remember, Mike was from Cleveland, and the old turkey trick made the news almost every year, but for some reason, Mike had never noticed it. So we jumped in my car and drove.

Now for those not familiar with the turkey trick, the thing is that it's all just a gag. There are no turkeys to be picked up. The directions we were given were completely bogus, leading to some obscure place over nonexistent roads looking for a nonexistent turkey farm. After driving around like idiots for a couple of hours, we figured out that we had been had. But we decided we weren't coming back empty-handed. We were going to have the last laugh. As we continued to drive around, we actually found a turkey farm. There were real live turkeys there. So we went up to the farmhouse and knocked.

"Hi," I said. "We're supposed to be out hunting turkeys today and have had no luck. But we don't want to come back home without a turkey. Could we buy one of those turkeys out there?"

The gentleman looked at us like we were screwballs. First off, in rural central Ohio, which is Amish country, you don't find very many black guys, especially those who claim to be turkey hunters while dressed in Adidas sweat suits and driving a white Jeep Cherokee. But hey, this was business, so the farmer agreed to sell us a live turkey.

We tossed that gobbling motherfucker in the back of my Cherokee and headed back to Berea. It took a couple hours to get back to Berea, and that damn turkey gobbled, clucked, and shit all over the back seat of my car. He wasn't too happy to be making the trip. Feathers stuck to the back seat for weeks.

Upon returning to our facility at Baldwin-Wallace College, I grabbed that squawking bird and took him into the locker room, tossing that feathery fucker on the floor. He got up and began running around, certainly bewildered as to where he was and what the hell he was doing here. He was turning into a pretty mean butterball bastard. But eventually Bobby Glenn, who managed our equipment room, caught him, took him home, and ate him.

This, by the way, is how Joe "Turkey" Jones got his name. He fell for the trick—twice! He drove all over, trying to find the place to get the turkeys, and kept calling the veterans for clarification of the directions. They of course just messed with him even more, but he kept trying. Eventually one of the veterans told him it was all bullshit and to just go home. But Turkey Jones didn't believe him and kept on trying to find those damn turkeys. Thus, he earned his feathers.

Joe was a helluva player—strong, quick, and a great pass rusher and pass blocker. Joe did two tours of duty with the Browns, from 1970 to 1973 and then again from 1975 to 1978. I didn't get there until 1981, but from the stories I heard, it sounds like he was awfully easy to mess with. (I don't know if there's a statistic for most offside penalties, but Joe would likely be right up there.) Once he went to Morrie Kono, the longtime equipment manager, to get a shoelace, and Morrie asked him if he needed the right one or left one. Joe went back to his locker to check.

CHAPTER SIX

Favorite Game #1: Browns vs. Steelers, Dec. 19, 1982

The weather randomly morphed from snow to sleet to rain. It was a balmy 34 degrees on this mid-December day. Brown water pooled on the mucky field. A perfect day for Browns football. Especially a Browns-Steelers game, with playoff implications on the line. I liked it when the weather was sloppy. It slowed down wide receivers and made it more difficult for them to makes their cuts and breaks. I could cover them tighter.

It already had been a difficult year. During the off-season, the Browns had traded away Lyle Alzado, Greg Pruitt, Robert L. Jackson, and Don Goode. Henry Sheppard walked out and subsequently retired. We won the season opener in Seattle, 21-7, and lost in the last minute to the Eagles in Week 2, 24-23. Then came the strike. It was painful, acrimonious and lasted 57 difficult days. We got back to work November 21 and beat the Patriots, 10-7, at the Stadium as Matt Bahr booted the winning field goal as time expired. But then we lost three in a row, and trouble was brewing all around.

Ricky Feacher called a players-only meeting early in the week.

The morning sports page was all abuzz about Paul McDonald's first NFL start. Despite his 71 straight starts, Brian Sipe had been inconsistent in the strike-shortened, nine-game 1982 season, and

Sam Rutigliano felt it was time to go to the bullpen. Brian told reporters after the win over New England, "I think I stunk." Our offense could muster only 47 points since the strike ended. We had
no touchdowns in the first half. It must have been very difficult for
Brian to watch this game from the sideline. But Sam had made a
calculated business decision, and Paul had earned his chance. Also
in the sports page, and on the lips of NBC analyst Merlin Olsen, was
an ominous foreshadowing—Sam, sporting a .500 record with the
Browns, now in his seventh season as coach and already fifth in se-
niority among NFL coaches—had better start producing a winner
or he "could be in trouble." *Plain Dealer* columnist Bob Dolgan said
that Sam's charm and humor "are the same factors that keep him
from the coaching pinnacle." In essence, Sam just didn't get mad
enough. "You have to be obsessed," Dolgan wrote.

What a pile of horsecrap. Blanton Collier was probably the most
phlegmatic personality in the history of coaching, yet his record
was tremendous. He was the absolute antithesis of high-strung
tough guys such as Paul Brown, Vince Lombardi, George Halas,
and Forrest Gregg. He's the last coach ever to lead the Browns to a
world title. So to say Sam didn't win enough because he didn't get
mad enough was just total shit. When the lockerroom doors were
closed and the media out of the room, Sam could get plenty mad.
He made your business his business. He knew everything about
you. You couldn't get away with anything under Sam.

We were 2-4 at this point, coming off those three straight losses
to Dallas, San Diego, and Cincinnati, but were still very much in the
playoff hunt due to the reconstituted 16-team playoff format adopted that year. And of all things, we were playing those goddamn
Steelers. They were 4-2 and needed a win to clinch a playoff spot.
They hadn't been to the playoffs in two years. They were coming
off their second shutout loss of the abbreviated season, a 13-0 loss
to Buffalo the previous week, which to date was Terry Bradshaw's
worst performance of his career. The perfect scenario had been set.

Well over 72,000 tickets had been sold for the game, but only

67,000 (many making the 2½-hour trek from Pittsburgh) braved the elements and showed up. Local television was blacked out. This was one of those rare times a Browns-Steelers game hadn't sold out. As usual, the Stadium was rocking. It always rocked for any AFC Central game, but it really rocked when the goddamn Steelers were in town.

Although I had nearly two seasons under my belt, I had yet to grab an interception. I came close a few times but still hadn't pulled one down. As I looked out at the gray, cold December day, I felt something special. Evidently, the Steelers did, too. In the NBC broadcast booth, Merlin Olsen said that the goddamn Steelers felt that I was "a man they feel they could take advantage of." I remember all too well how those goddamn Steelers passed on me in the draft because they thought I was too short. Payback and punishment were in order.

The Steelers, celebrating the 50th year of their franchise, featured future Hall of Famers Terry Bradshaw, Franco Harris, Lynn Swann, John Stallworth, "Iron Mike" Webster—monsters, all of them. Mean Joe Greene and L.C. Greenwood had just retired. And while we had had our woes winning in Pittsburgh, they had had their troubles over the years in Cleveland. Much was made over our inability to win at Three Rivers Stadium, but the Steelers didn't win a game in Cleveland from 1964 to 1974.

Much has been said over the years about Franco Harris's running style. The rap on him was that he supposedly would hit the line and then run for the sideline. I didn't see any evidence of that. He was more of a finesse runner than a power runner, yes, and he knew what he had to do to prolong his great career. He didn't shy away from contact when the situation arose. He might not have sought out contact like Earl Campbell, but Campbell will pay a dear price for the rest of his life. The poor guy had three vertebrae removed from his spine. He can hardly walk.

I charged down the field covering the opening kickoff and rammed my head on the ball, popping it loose from Fred Bohannon. The Steelers recovered it, but that was a thrilling start. We held the Steelers in check, and after they punted, Matt Bahr connected on a 44-yarder in the muck. Kicking a field goal that long in those conditions should have been worth four points.

Nonetheless, we had to take care of business. Bradshaw, who had more touchdown passes against the Browns than anyone in history, had the Steelers on the march in the first quarter, and floated a pass right over me into the hands of Jim Smith. Just missed again. I had the inside position of the pattern covered perfectly but just couldn't locate the ball in time.

Three plays later, Bradshaw tried to hit Stallworth on the left side. He and Larry "Bobo" Braziel, aptly nicknamed for the professional wrestler, leapt for it jump-ball style, and Braziel won the tip, knocking the ball as high as Bo Derek's cheekbones. It seemed as though I could have read the Sunday paper and prepared my taxes before that damn ball came down into my hands as I dragged both feet just inside the north sideline at our 8. I jumped in the air and yelled. I had my first NFL interception. Clarence Scott jumped on me. As did Bob Golic. So did Eddie Johnson. All those laps. All those damn back-and-forth drills in the asphyxiating Mississippi August air. All those weights. All those film sessions. All those hits. Finally, that fucking prolate spheroid was in my hands. My first interception. I ran to the sideline and gave the ball to our equipment manager, Bobby Glenn, to put it away for me. Being only a second-year player, it was quite an honor to get the reaction I did among the veterans. Interception number one was now in the books, but it would take two more years for me to get my first fumble recovery.

That ball and the other 25 interceptions I snagged during my career are in cases in my sister's house. I would send them to her and to my parents. After my mother died, Debra collected all of them. One day, someone offered her $10,000 for the whole lot, and Debra said no deal. In fact, she won't even let me have them! She certainly has been one of my top fans all along.

Our offense continued to do very little. Numerous passes were dropped, including some very well-thrown long balls by Paul, a southpaw. Paul hit Dan Fulton for a 50-yard gain, but a holding penalty brought that back. Mike Pruitt, our best mudder, went out with a thigh bruise, and Cleo Miller filled in, teaming up with Heisman Trophy winner Charles White in the backfield. In the second quarter, Bradshaw had them on the march again, and on third-and-goal from our 6, he fired one for Stallworth in the front corner of the end zone. I was covering Jim Smith a few yards up but saw the ball coming, spun around and reached for it—but it sailed just over my outstretched hand and into Stallworth's awaiting breadbasket as I splashed facedown in the muck. Just missed another one, and those goddamn Steelers had a touchdown. Shit.

We got the ball on the kickoff, and Paul tried to hit Dan again on a long ball down the left side. But Mel Blount, the oldest man on the goddamn Steelers, read the play perfectly and came up with the 53rd interception of his great career, setting the all-time Steelers record. That gave the ball back to Bradshaw with just over a minute left in the half.

Then the goddamn Steelers got two big, cheesy penalties against us. Clinton Burrell was called for interference, then Chip Banks was called for roughing the passer. I protested loudly to the refs on both of those calls, to no avail. So we decided we'd have a surprise for the goddamn Steelers on the next play.

In the defensive huddle, the call came for me to come in on a corner blitz, known as the Rover Blitz. I assessed the situation as the Steelers broke the huddle and lined up. Smith was over me, and if he released, I would have a clean shot into the backfield. I cheated a bit to the inside, leading with my left foot, but was still careful to disguise my intentions. Clarence also came up and covered his man tightly. On the snap, I released Smith downfield. Bradshaw took six steps back and looked to his right. That meant Bradshaw was looking away from me, and there was no one in the way to stop me even if Bradshaw had faded back to Ashtabula. Those back shoulders were open and square, and my eyes grew as wide as those of a tomcat seeing a female alley cat turn around and lift her tail. Unimpeded, I accelerated over eight steps and drilled my facemask right between his shoulder blades. Bradshaw crumpled to the ground in a bald-headed mud pile, and the ball fluttered away. Elvis Franks jumped on it and tried to get up for what probably would have been an easy score, but he couldn't get any traction. Still, I got the sack (one of only two in my nine-year career) and forced the fumble, and the goddamn Steelers' attempt to mount another scoring drive had been thwarted. What a great call by Marty.

That was certainly a great hit, but by today's rules I would have been penalized. We used to be taught to explode through the ball carrier's body with your headgear, but nowadays that's considered spearing.

The turning point of the game came about two-thirds through the third quarter. A Steve Cox punt splattered dead in the mud at the goddamn Steelers' 6, and we held them to a three-and-out. John Goodson, one of these screwy barefooted kickers (remember, it was raining and 34 degrees) then shanked a punt out of bounds for 16 yards. McDonald then hit Ozzie on a 22-yard play down the left sideline, beating Donnie Shell. Now it was time for Johnny "B-1 Bomber" Davis to do his thing. The Browns had signed him just two weeks before. Twice, he charged headfirst into what was left of the now rusty Steel Curtain, tightly clutching the ball with his powerful but sleek piano-playing hands (He was a great piano player, despite never having a lesson). The second time, he slipped through for a 1-yard touchdown.

We now led, 10-7, and it was going to be another Kardiac-style fourth quarter. Old pro Clarence Scott, whom I called "The Glue" because he always kept things together, got things started off right by pilfering Bradshaw on the first play. We failed to capitalize, and Bradshaw tried another pass across the middle. I saw the play develop, reacted to it, broke to the middle, and the ball hit me square in the hands. Interception number two. Or so I thought. The soggy ball slipped through my hands and feebly fell into the muck. Damn.

With just over five minutes remaining, the goddamn Steelers got the ball again. Big runs by Harris and Frank Pollard, along with a catch by Smith when I slipped in the mud, put the goddamn Steelers on our 39. But Smith barely missed a pass from Bradshaw, and the goddamn Steelers were looking at fourth-and-4 with just over a minute to go. That would have been a 56-yard field goal attempt for Gary Anderson, but with the field being an acre of mashed-up, green-and-brown pig slop, that would have been a herculean feat. So the goddamn Steelers went for it. Bradshaw gunned a pass on the right side for Swann, who had not caught a pass all day. I saw it coming, but Bradshaw didn't see me. I dove in front of Swann and snagged the ball. Interception number two, and this time, I held on to it. I hit the ground and bounced up. Some of my teammates, and I for that matter, didn't know if I had been touched down or if the play was still on. Chip Banks reached over to give me a congratulatory swat on the helmet, and I ran around in a circle before being knocked down by a very pissed off Mike Webster. I ran to the sideline and gave the ball to Bobby to stash it away with the other trophy.

We ran the clock down as far as we could but wound up with a fourth down on our 11 with 13 seconds to go. Cox took the punt snap and ran around as much as he could before stepping over the end line for an intentional safety. A fair catch on the ensuing free kick gave the goddamn Steelers one more shot. Everyone remembers the "Immaculate Reception" playoff game between these goddamn Steelers and the Raiders 10 years before, when Harris picked a batted pass off his shoe top and ran it in on a fourth-down desperation play. There's even a fucking bronze statue in the Pittsburgh airport of Harris catching that ball. But history was not going to repeat itself today. Bradshaw tried to hit Smith over the right side, but I was there again. Unlike the great Jack Tatum, who knocked the ball away and into Harris's hands on that infamous play, I grabbed interception number three to complete the hat trick, and the game was over.

Someone forgot to remind those goddamn Steelers that I was too goddamn short to play for them. Three interceptions, a sack and two forced fumbles. Put up a gold statue of that in your stupid airport, you motherfuckers.

Paul had outperformed the Hall of Fame-bound Bradshaw, hitting on 19 of 40 passes for 227 yards and just one interception. Not bad, considering the weather and field conditions. His numbers could have been substantially better had several soggy passes not been dropped. After the game, Sam affirmed Paul's status as the starter for next week's game against Houston. However, next season, Brian came to camp and won the starting job back. Rookies Dwight Walker (whose career was most unfortunately cut short by an auto wreck), and Mike Whitwell made some big plays at crucial points during the game. Bob Golic had replaced Henry Bradley at nose tackle two weeks earlier and came up with some big defensive stops for us as well. Game balls were given to the four defensive coaches.

Bradshaw told the media, "This was about my most frustrating loss ever." We had contained the great Franco Harris, who already had established an NFL record for rushing attempts and was chasing Jim Brown's NFL rushing record of 12,312 yards. Harris, whose two longest touchdown runs of his career (75 and 71 yards) came against the Browns, did have a tendency to hit the hole and angle to the sidelines, a technique that irritated Jim. Brown jokingly talked about coming out of retirement at age 47 to reset his record if Harris had broken it. Jim was never serious about it, but the media played it up as if he would really try it. Even Art said Jim would be welcome to come to camp and try to make the team legitimately. But it was all a ruse. Jim never intended to play another down. Harris retired after 13 seasons with 12,120 yards, 192 shy of Jim's record, set in nine 14-game seasons.

As we sat around in the locker room and peeled off our mud-soaked uniforms, Sam walked behind me and gave me a whack on the back of the head.

"It's about time you did something right," he quipped.

We went to Houston the following week, knowing we'd have to face Earl Campbell and company the day after Christmas. Tackling Earl is like tackling a runaway truck. But we stuffed him like a Christmas goose with our special brand of holiday cheer, holding the "Tyler Rose" to 43 yards, and even caused him to fumble twice—once near our goal line and once by their goal line late in the game. Clinton Burrell recovered both fumbles and we beat the Oilers, 20-14. But the following week, we lost to those goddamn Steelers in Pittsburgh on the final weekend of the regular season. We finished with a 4-5 record, but thanks to a New England victory over Buffalo and the conference record tiebreaker, we, along with Detroit, became the first teams with losing records to make the playoffs.

Things didn't work out well for us in the playoffs, as we had to go up against the top-seeded L.A. Raiders. On the plane ride to Los Angeles, there was a lot of commotion in the front of the plane, and someone was lying down in the aisle. I heard Sam say, "Oh no, it's Art." Art had had some sort of cardiac episode. When the plane landed about 30 minutes later, Art was taken by ambulance to a hospital. Sam went with him. Art pulled through, but he needed a cardiac catheterization, which he had kept putting off.

We lost the playoff game, 27-10. It was close in the first half, but the Raiders pulled away later. The Raiders then lost to the Dolphins, who then lost to the Redskins in the Super Bowl.

During my career we were 11-7 against the goddamn Steelers. There was just something about these games with the goddamn Steelers that brought out my best. In 1984 I would pick off two in a game at Three Rivers. Not bad for a midget.

CHAPTER SEVEN

Frank Minnifield, Co-Dawg

It's the night of January 3, 1986. We're in Miami, the night before
the playoff game with the Dolphins. We had gotten beat down by
the Jets the week before but backed into first place with an 8-8 record. Frank and I were rooming on the road, preparing for the big
game the next day. I needed to be comfortable, so I turned the thermostat down in the hotel room. After a few minutes, I noticed it was
getting warmer, not cooler in the room.

Frank had decided he needed to be comfortable, too, so he
turned the thermostat up.

"What the fuck are you doing, Boom?" I yelled. We called each
other "Boom" all the time. How that got started, I'm not sure.

"It's too damn cold in here," Frank retorted.

"The hell it is," I snapped back. "Turn that heat off."

"No way," Frank maintained. "Got to have it warm in here."

"Fuck no. It's too hot."

"Fuck yes, it's too damn cold."

But I then reminded Frank of our agreement. On the road we
alternated which way the room was going to be. I liked it cool, and
with the TV on all night. Frank liked it warm, with the TV off. But
this was my week, so I prevailed. Out of frustration, Frank pulled
the mattress off his bed, grabbed a blanket and pillow, and dragged
them all into the bathroom. He threw everything in the tub and
closed the door. And there he stayed until morning. He slept the

night in the fucking bathtub. One might think that would have ill effects on our ability to play the next day. Well, against the great Dan Marino, I allowed one reception. Frank allowed none.

*   *   *

Born in Lexington, Kentucky, on January 1, 1960, Frank grew up following the Browns, and he played for Henry Clay High School in Lexington. But at only 5-9 and 140 pounds, he was considered too small to play college ball. That didn't deter "Mighty Minnie." He walked on at the University of Louisville and earned a scholarship his last three years.

Frank's specialty was kick returns—he led the nation with a 30.4 average on kickoff returns in 1981. Being uncertain of where he might end up in the NFL Draft, Frank signed with the Chicago Blitz of the upstart USFL after they drafted him in the third round. The Browns had him pegged for a second-round pick in the NFL Draft.

Frank was confident in his new coach, former great Redskins coach George Allen, and the defensive scheme that was in place. Then, in the opening game of his rookie year, Frank tore up his knee. He missed the remainder of the season.

The Blitz later moved to Arizona to become the Arizona Wranglers, and in 1984 the Wranglers won the USFL title. Meanwhile, Frank wanted to come to the NFL.

Five teams in the NFL were bidding for his services. The money was pretty much the same from all five, but Frank liked the defensive scheme we had in Cleveland. Sam Rutigliano and the scouts liked what they saw in Frank, but Art Modell was hesitant. He even asked the advice of Oakland/Los Angeles Raiders owner Al Davis. Davis told Art to forget about Frank—he was just too short. But Sam convinced Art that Frank would give us some much-needed support at corner, and Art ponied up a series of four one-year contracts, reportedly worth about $1.6 million, with $400,000 guaranteed. That was better money than Donnie Rogers and I were making, both of us being first-round draft choices, and Frank had yet to play a down in our league. Since Frank and I both were vocal and aggressive leaders, the possibility existed that we might get along as well as a couple of red roosters.

"With two number-one draft picks and me as a high-priced free agent, we could have problems," Frank told *The Plain Dealer*. But he went out of his way to get to know all of the defensive backs, and it was clear that he meant business. We all chose to hang together and to get along. We got to know each other, each other's family situations, each other's struggles and triumphs. The importance of chemistry on a team simply cannot be understated.

Frank had played in 15 games of the 20-game USFL season, which started in the spring, intercepting four passes, recovering two fumbles, and blocking a couple of kicks. Plus he was nursing a strained arch. We didn't want to work him in too fast. But before he could put the pads on, the Wranglers sent a letter to Frank that arrived the same day he arrived at our camp, claiming they still had an option year him for 1985; thus he couldn't sign with any other team.

For a month, Frank couldn't do much more than just watch practice from the sidelines. He returned to Lexington while the legal haranguing went back and forth. But as the bids for Frank came in, the Wranglers made a crucial error. They offered him $900,000 to stay, which the court later interpreted as meaning the Wranglers weren't picking up his option. Why would they offer him $900,000 if they had an option on him for $90,000? On August 22, 1984, Jefferson County (Kentucky) Circuit Court Judge William McAnulty issued a restraining order against the Wranglers, ordering them not to interfere with Frank's negotiations with the Browns. Frank was activated a few days before our regular-season opener—a debacle in Seattle. He became a starter in Week 4, a 20-10 win over those goddamn Steelers, and our first victory of what would be a tumultuous season.

*   *   *

Frank might not have had the great size, but he made up for it with his speed (4.4 in the 40-yard dash) and tremendous leaping ability, an NBA-worthy 44-inch vertical leap that earned him the nickname "Sky." He also possessed tremendous balance—he could dish out a hit or take a hit and still be square on his feet. His tremendous acceleration gave him the ability to close down on a receiver quickly—the ball would have to be thrown absolutely perfectly to get through. It didn't take long to realize that Frank and I had something very special. He was a natural fit. With his aggressiveness and closing speed, we both could play bump-and-run with the best wide receivers in the league, taking the "scoundrels of the earth," as Frank described them, out of the game. That left the quarterbacks with less time and fewer options, and let the rest of the defense concentrate on interior and underneath coverages. We hated zone coverage—and we hardly ever went to it.

While Frank was known for using a computer to study opposing receivers, I was the one who got him into it. When Marty was defensive backfield coach, he always got on me about preparation, saying that even though I had a lot of talent, I could play a bit better if I spent more time on preparation. I convinced Frank of that as well. He went on to keep a record of every receiver in the league with his big, clanky computer. This was the mid-1980s, long before lightweight laptops, notebooks, and tablets. Computers were cumbersome.

Frank studied those scoundrels with professorial analytical intensity, often while the rest of us were snoozing on the plane. He would show me and others tendencies and cues he picked up. Often we would even review the data and videos at halftime. I can't overstate the importance of film study. It enabled us to anticipate and play receivers better. I kept stacks of manila folders in my condo filled with notes on the habits and tendencies of opposing receivers. Other cornerbacks around the league often watched what Frank did with opposing receivers and incorporated his techniques into their personal defensive game plans.

I, on the other hand, was more vocal and excitable. Sam Rutigliano once described the difference in styles between Frank and me this way: "Minnifield was a great little competitor, a smart guy. Dixon was a pain in the ass." I think that was a compliment. Doug Looney of *Sports Illustrated* described us as "two of the orneriest, cockiest, brashest—and don't forget best—cornerbacks in the league. Schottenheimer says he wouldn't trade them for any pair in the NFL. Every time there's action, these guys seem to be a part of it."

Like me, Frank loved to yak at the receivers. We yakked about everything. We made fun of their shoes, their uniforms, called them slow and ugly, and told them how great their mother was last night, and that their girlfriend was a whore. We did everything to get into their heads, to distract them, and to make them think about anything else but what they were supposed to do.

Every Sunday afternoon, we didn't like you because of your looks, your team, your mother, your ethnicity, your school—everything and anything that would give us a reason to knock a player out of the game. Several of us would often get together and pitch in on a pool and essentially put a bounty on certain opponents. The object wasn't to maim or cause serious injury, but to knock him out of the game. These pools would be maybe a couple hundred bucks, not really that much money.

The NFL caused a bit of a ruckus in 2012 when it disclosed evidence of bounty-hunting organized by one of the assistant coaches of the New Orleans Saints. But here's the news on that news: It wasn't news. As Captain Renault in *Casablanca* said about Rick's Café, with feigned surprise, "I am shocked, *shocked* to find that gambling in going on in here" (while collecting his winnings). Bounty-hunting has been going on in the league for years. For decades. And not just in the NFL, but in the NBA and NHL as well.

Hockey teams often a have certain players known as "goons" whose main job is to start a fight with someone on the other team, the purpose of which is to cause the opposing team to have to play with one of its better players sitting in the penalty box for five (or more) minutes. Charles Barkley and Cedric Maxwell have told of bounty-hunting in the NBA. Barkley said while he was playing for the Philadelphia 76ers, a $5,000 bounty was posted for taking out opposing players who continued to take 3-point shots during a blowout. Cedric Maxwell even named the Celtics' target: Len Elmore. "One time, we were getting beat by 30 points, back, this was in my Philadelphia days,"

Barkley said on *The Dan Patrick Show*. "I'm a firm believer if a guy shoots a 3 (during a blowout) that you knock his ass as far in the stands as you possibly can. We were getting beat by 30 or 40, I can't remember, and this guy was shooting 3s and running up and down the court, and I said, 'Hey, we got to hurt that guy right there.'"

Maxwell, who played in the NBA for 11 seasons, the first eight with the Celtics, told WBZ-TV in Boston, "We did it in the NBA. We had a guy, Len Elmore, used to love to take charges. He's an analyst right now for CBS. You might want to hear this, Len. We had a bounty on you. If you stepped on his chest, you got paid. It was about $10, but it was enough. [Elmore] was wondering why guys were stepping on him . . . Not taking him out; just putting an imprint on his chest, the size of my shoe."

I don't know if it's as common in baseball, but I wouldn't be surprised if there were under-the-table bonuses for a timely beanball or spiking of a particularly annoying opponent. Certainly it would be bad business for coaches to officially sanction it. But it was commonplace.

I don't know whether any of our coaches were aware of it, but if they were, they quietly filed it away under "Don't ask, don't tell." Our bounty-hunting was informal, more out of fun, and it was never our intention to maim an opponent or end his season. We just wanted to knock him out the game, just that game, and with a strictly legal hit. Remember now, the Browns' administration of that era is now in Baltimore, so if any of you directors of football etiquette at the league office have an issue with this, call the Ravens.

"Those two were the best competitors I ever went up against," Denver wide receiver Steve Watson said of Frank and me. "I tried to do everything I could to get in their heads and piss them off. I'd go after them and try to cut them, but they'd just jump on my back all pissed off. They were probably the two most physical guys I had to deal with."

I guess you could say we were "Dawgs, The Bounty Hunters" long before that *Dog The Bounty Hunter* show that's now on TV.

One of the more infamous moments happened in the 14th game of the 1984 season. Cris "Cadillac" Collinsworth of the Bengals was a quick, tall, flashy wide receiver. Drafted in the second round the same year I was drafted, he already had been to the Pro Bowl three times. No question, this guy was talented, and this particular afternoon, the Dawgs were out for him.

You see, Cadillac was a cute, little, golden, white boy playing a black man's position. Yes, that sounds racist, but, like I said, on Sunday afternoons, if being a racist for three hours made me a better, tougher player, then so be it. Cadillac came streaking across the field like greased white lightning, and Frank blasted him, grinding Captain Snowflake to the ground in a heap. We danced around him like Indians around a campfire while he lay as motionless as a dead white bass floating down the murky waters of the Cuyahoga River.

"That's what you get for coming across our spot," we yelled at him. We caught some flack for that, but, we had done nothing illegal. He was hit hard and clean, and that's they way we do business in the NFL. If you don't like it, don't cut across our zone—or go sell Amway.

Despite Collinsworth being knocked out of the game, the Bengals rallied in the fourth quarter. Down by a touchdown, the Bengals blocked a punt because of a blocking assignment screwup with just over a minute left. Then with 19 seconds left, Boomer Esiason tried to hit another cute little white boy, Steve Kreider, in the end zone. I wasn't going to let that happen but got too aggressive and got nailed for interference. That gave the Bengals a first down on the 1, and on the next play, Esiason hit Anthony Munoz on a tackle-eligible pass for the tying score. They went on to win in overtime, 20-17.

Now don't get the wrong impression. And you book review writers, don't take what I've written out of context. I can see the headlines now: Dixon calls Collinsworth "Captain Snowflake." Get it right. For two Sundays a year, for three hours each, he was Captain Snowflake, or worse. Remember, we did everything we could to get into opponents' heads during the game, but afterward, it was over. I have nothing but the greatest respect for anyone—of any background or ethnicity—who has the talent and courage to play in the NFL. Collinsworth was a helluva player and a brilliant man. He now provides color commentary on television and holds a law degree.

During the game, we were nasty, mean, chippy, full of ourselves and just plain didn't like you. We were racists, bigots, homophobes, anti-Semitic, anti-whatever you were. We hollered at the refs, the opposing coaches and, yes, we clutched, grabbed, scratched, pushed and held as much as we could get away with. It was our job to intimidate and hit the wrong-colored jerseys as hard as we were physically and legally able to, or at least what we were able to get away with. That's the NFL. But afterward, we were all brothers, even though we didn't fraternize with opposing wide receivers.

Captain Snowflake knew we were as tough as they come. He once said of us, "They are as good as anybody. They have different styles, but both are very effective. All I can say is that I give both of them my votes for Pro Bowl every year. And that's as big a compliment as we can pay them. I came into this league with Hanford Dixon and he's gotten better every year."

Another tough snowflake who gave us grief was Seattle's Steve Largent. He wasn't all that fast, but as tough as they make them. He had a tremendous instinct of when to cut, and his patterns were precise. He had great hands, and when he got the ball, he ran with the power of a fullback. Frank and I hated covering him. I found it a bit too coincidental before one game against the Seahawks that

Frank came up to me just before the game and began complaining of a tightening hamstring. How convenient.

Largent went on to have one of the most prolific careers of any wide receiver. He appeared in seven Pro Bowls and held just about every receiving record at the time of his retirement. He then served four terms in the U.S. House of Representatives, representing a district in the Tulsa, Oklahoma, region and never receiving less than 60 percent of the vote.

I pushed the limits with the officials, too. I yelled and yakked at them, peppered with plenty of heat-of-the-moment profanity. I knew how far to take it. When they gave me a certain look I would knock it off and head back to the huddle before they could reach for the yellow hankie. Knowing the intensity of the game and of the moment, most officials would let you vent as long as you didn't get too much in their face and knew when to turn around and get back to your team. But after the game, even the more intense games where I got at the refs quite a bit, I'd still tell them, "Good game," even crack a smile at them. They have a tough, thankless job where they take it in one ear from one sideline and in the other ear from the other sideline, and from intense, cocky, know-it-alls like me.

I got a kick out of a comical meeting between NFL Commissioner Pete Rozelle and the great Jack Tatum. Tatum had the rightly earned reputation for being a fierce hitter, but his reputation for being a cheap-shot artist was overstated and mostly a media creation. Tatum, of course, is probably best known for the hit he delivered on Patriots wide receiver Darryl Stingley in an exhibition game in 1978 that paralyzed Stingley from the neck down for the rest of his life. In April 2007, Stingley died from complications of being a quadriplegic. Certainly that was tragic, but Tatum's hit on Stingley was clean and legal, and in reality, wasn't really that hard. You can look it up on YouTube. Stingley and Tatum just hit at the most inopportune angle, and it was more of a freak accident than a vicious hit. An inch or two higher or lower, or at a slightly different angle, it could have just as easily been Tatum's neck that was broken.

Tatum was summoned to Rozelle's office in the fall of 1976, two years before the Stingley incident, to discuss his rough-and-tumble play, and Rozelle delivered a line of unintentional comic genius, as Tatum retold it in his infamous book, *They Call Me Assassin.*

"Jack," Rozelle said, "I personally think you hit too hard."

Yep. Rozelle wasn't saying Tatum was cheap-shotting anybody. He was just hitting "too hard." Yeah, and Tony Dorsett just ran too damn fast. No fair.

Tatum, though, had the brilliant comeback.

"Mr. Commissioner, Earl Campbell weighs 235 pounds. He runs a 9.6 hundred, each one of his thighs is 34 inches of thick hard muscle . . . ah, really, I don't want to be a wise guy, but how would you tackle him easy?"

Tatum was dead-on right. Frank and I had had enough experience getting our damn necks tangled between those twisting and churning 34-inch steel cables as Campbell ran like a spooked wild steer escaping a Texas slaughterhouse. I thought about the more sensitive, gentle approach, but he didn't seem the type.

The NFL was and still is a league of large, aggressive men playing a very physical sport with millions of dollars at stake. If you didn't play hard, run hard, and hit hard, you were a victim. Tatum knew that, I knew that, Frank knew that—hell, everyone in this racket has known that. And that includes those Look-At-Me-I'm-Hot-Shit wide receivers who dared to tread upon our turf.

Physical risk we voluntarily undertook in our quest for glory, fame and *money.* Fuck all this black-and-white celluloid "for the love of the game" bullshit romanticism. It was never like that and never will be. Like Tatum, Frank and I were paid to hit and hit hard. We were paid to stop you any way we could within the rules, or at least around the edges of the rules. And that's what we did. No excuses, no apologies. In this game, and especially at this level, you have to go 100 percent on every play. The day you let up and don't hit the other guy with everything you've got is the day you get hurt, replaced, or released—or any combination of the three.

And Tatum, as tough as he was, certainly wasn't the first, last, or only player to punish the opposition. He was just the first one to write a book about it.

In its earlier days, football was a much more brutal game than it is today. There were no rules about bumping receivers downfield. If the runner was down, he wasn't really down until his momentum was stopped. Thus, he could get up and keep running, and defenders would deliver an extra shot while he was on the ground to keep him there. The flying wedge was an absolute meat grinder. Hardy Brown, who played in the 1940s and '50s, took advantage of the lack of facemasks and drove his shoulder pads into opponents' faces every chance he got. He was just plain crazy and wound up dying in a mental institution. Realizing the futility of going strength on strength with Jim Brown, defenders often went for Brown's eyes. As tough and rough as the game is today, it's girlie-ball compared to what it was a generation ago.

Frank and I brought our intensity to practice as well. Normally, the first-team offense would practice against the scout defense— the defensive scheme used by the upcoming opponents. Few starting defenders were on the scout team. But Frank and I would jump in and tell the scout cornerbacks to take a seat. We wanted to toughen up our technique and toughen up our receiver corps.

Our receivers would have to go up against the likes of Lester "The Molester" Hayes and Mike Haynes of the L.A. Raiders, the duo to which Frank and I were often compared. Hayes was known for his low, crouching stance and for coating himself with Stickum, which the league banned in 1981. He was also a huge *Star Wars* fan, often declaring in interviews that he was the "only true Jedi" in the NFL. Haynes, a Hall of Famer, was the fifth overall pick in the 1976 draft and split his career between the Patriots and the Raiders.

Those guys were tough and nasty, so we practiced tough and nasty on our receivers. They thought they were pretty tough, but they weren't. They were wide receivers, paid and trained to run away from guys. We were paid and trained to run into them and deliver punishing blows. This resulted in fights breaking out almost every practice. We egged them on, got in their pansy faces and busted up their carefully planned routes. Brian Brennan and Frank seemed to get into it every day. Those battles were epic.

I had my fair share of scuffles with Webster Slaughter and Reggie Langhorne. I mean, we had nasty, hockey-style fights where we each pulled the other guy's jersey over his head. We had this one drill where Reggie would come at me and block, and my job was to shed him and get to the ball carrier. Reggie was taller than me, so one time, instead of just pushing him aside, I bent my knees and extended my arms upward, catching him underneath the front of the shoulder pads. Reggie went flying—*whump*—back on his head and bony ass. He jumped up, acting or thinking he was tougher than I, and it was on. Just a typical day at the office for us. But it never got too far out of hand. Inevitably, someone would step in and separate us—the last thing anyone wanted was for someone to break a hand while stupidly punching the other guy in the facemask.

It never spilled into the locker room. We all knew we were brothers in arms, always having each other's back. While at the moment they didn't appreciate what we were doing to them, they realized that it indeed was making them tougher and better. We fought and loved each other like crazed adolescent siblings. And come Sunday, we went into battle—together.

The results speak for themselves—Reggie and Webster were constant deep threats for whom opposing defenses had to account, and Brian was quick, sure-handed, smart, and had that knack for ping-ponging his way through the bruising maze of shoulder pads, forearms, and elbows to the head to come up with those clutch third-down catches. And there was future Hall of Famer Ozzie Newsome, a tight end with wide receiver speed, cutting through seams in the zones and coming up with those wizard-like catches. Add to that Bernie Kosar's cool and cerebral manner and laser-accurate throws, and the 1-2 punch of Kevin Mack and Earnest Byner in the backfield, and it was no wonder the Browns were the most exciting team of the 1980s.

*   *   *

Frank and I had our pregame routines and rituals. If it was a road game, it would start at the airport. We would fly to the destination city on Saturday, unless it was a West Coast game. For those we would leave on Friday in order to better adjust to the time difference. On the plane, the rookies provided us with Popeye's fried chicken. When we arrived at the destination airport, the guys as well as the coaches would fight among themselves to ride whichver bus Frank and I were taking to the hotel. We put on comedy shows, walking up and down the aisle, messing with everyone. We made fun of anybody and everybody, talked about their ugly clothes, a play they screwed up, a phobia that haunts them, what their girlfriend thinks of them—nothing was sacred. We had everyone in hysterics.

On the road, we had a mandatory team meal Saturday evening. I always had a Top Dawg Burger. If it was a home game, I had it at Tony Roma's. On the road, I had the hotel chef prepare one. Three patties with bacon, cheese, mayo, and egg. It carried me to the game. Then later on Saturday night, I would start to drink this green shit that trainer Bill Tessendorf provided. It was some green powder to which I added water. I have no idea what was in it, but it tasted OK. I never ate a pregame meal. I needed to have the strength of a lion and the speed of a deer, so I didn't want anything to weigh me down. The green powder drink did me just fine. It kept me from cramping up late in the game.

On Sunday, game day, we had chapel in the morning, which was optional, but I still liked to go. It helped me get a bit more focused.

I would typically arrive at the stadium somewhere between 9 and 9:30 a.m. for a 1 p.m. kickoff. I wanted to make sure I had plenty of time to get ready at my own pace and get my ankles taped by Mark Smith, the assistant trainer. I preferred his method of taping. Leo Murphy was a great trainer and had been with the ball club for decades, but I felt that Mark taped me up at just the right tension.

Taping too tightly can result in a reduction of circulation in the feet, and that would certainly be problematic for a defensive back.

Frank and I would get "spatted." That is, we would have our ankles taped outside the socks. It just gave us a bit more support and comfort, and spared us the agony of getting our lower leg hairs yanked out when you pulled the tape off. Often after getting taped, we would walk around the locker room just wearing our jocks—"spats and chaps," as we would say—or sometimes "socks and jocks." I would often have a Walkman on, listening to the Isley Brothers or P-Funk. I would zone in. Frank would walk around and just fuck with everyone. We walked around in our spats and chaps to show everyone that if you're more concerned with what you were wearing, your mind wasn't on the game.

"You ready to go, Boom? You ready to go to war, Boom?" he asked everyone, knocking the more inattentive ones upside the head.

I was once grooving around to some "It's a Disco Night" by the Isley Brothers in my spats and chaps when Marty called me into his office.

"What's going on?" he asked. "Are you high on something? You're acting weird." That actually hurt my feelings a bit.

"No, not at all, Coach. Just trying to zone in and focus. You know I always act weird before the game." Marty didn't argue.

Frank and I would finish getting dressed, pulling the back of each other's jersey down into position. I'd tuck in a long towel on my right hip. That would let me wipe the sweat off my face without having to bend over. Plus I liked the way it felt as it flapped like a flag as I ran. I thought it looked cool. We'd then head out on the field and walk around, checking the footing and field conditions, and interacting with the early-arriving Dawg Pound a bit at home games.

Frank and I also had our special celebration dance. We would start from opposite sides and run right at each other, leaping to the sky for a high-10 in the center of the field. I have photographic proof that my vertical leap was better than his.

*   *   *

In 1987, 1988, and 1989, Frank and I both made the Pro Bowl, and became the only corners from the same team to start. No other cornerback tandem had made it to the Pro Bowl more than once. Gary Green and LeRoy Irvin of the Rams made it in 1985. Jimmy Johnson and Bruce Taylor of the 49ers made it in 1971. I made the Pro Bowl in 1987, but not because of any great statistics. I had only three interceptions. But that's not bad, considering the fact that opposing quarterbacks only threw seven damn passes my way all year. That's a pretty fucking good batting average.

Frank and I should have been in the Pro Bowl earlier, but the fact that we called opponents every name in the book may have hurt our cause. It's the players who vote! We didn't have that many interceptions, but that was because we almost always ran the bump-and-run, which would take those receivers out of the play, making the quarterback throw to a secondary receiver who was trying to crack the seams. That would give more interception opportunities to the safeties and linebackers.

NFL Films did a video ranking the all-time great cornerback duos. We came in second, behind Hayes and Haynes of the Raiders. Often I am asked if Frank and/or I should be in the Hall of Fame. I would have to say yes. Three years in the Pro Bowl together—that has never happened before or since. Had we won a couple of Super Bowls, then I think we would have made it by now.

"I'd put them number one," Bengals quarterback Boomer Esiason said of us. "I played against them so much every year, twice a year. Between them and the Dawg Pound, Cleveland was one of the most difficult places and team to play against." He told about how during practice Bengals head coach Sam Wyche would yell at his receivers, "They're going to eat you up, they're going to take you down."

Esiason said, "Those two guys would push the contact rules to the absolute letter. If they were to play today, they wouldn't be playing, because there would be a flag on every play."

"They were in many ways the personality of that defense," added Hall of Famer and broadcaster Dan Dierdorf.

Michael Silver of Yahoo Sports said, "They weren't dominant because of their athletic greatness, they were dominant because of their mental will."

I was named a starter in the Pro Bowl after the 1987 season, and Frank was named to the special teams by Marty, who coached the AFC squad. When we got to Honolulu, Frank and I kind of went in opposite directions. I enjoyed hanging around with the other players, but Frank was kind of a hermit. He just didn't like hanging around with everyone. That's fine, to each his own.

Frank also made it to the Pro Bowl after the 1990 season, the year after I retired. But Frank's career was winding down much like it started—in legal entanglements.

The then-Plan B free-agency plan instituted by the league in 1988 allowed each team to protect 37 players each year, with the rest becoming free agents. When Frank's contract with the Browns expired in 1989, he sought offers from other teams. Despite four Pro Bowl appearances, no offers came. Frank, along with seven other players around the league, filed a lawsuit claiming that the Plan B compensation system amounted to collusion among the owners to hold salaries down. The suit was unsuccessful, and Frank did re-sign with the Browns three games into the 1990 season for $700,000, which increased to $800,000 in 1991, well below the $1 million per year he had been seeking. He felt he had no other choice. Frank played his last game December 27, 1992, in a 23-13 loss at Pittsburgh. The Browns did not offer him a contract the following year, stating that the competitive needs and the direction that the organization was going precluded any further need of his services at any price.

Frank finished his career with 20 interceptions and seven fumble recoveries. He also had three touchdowns (I had none), two on blocked punt returns, and an interception return for a score against the Indianapolis Colts in the divisional playoffs during the

1987 season. The Hall of Fame voters named him to the All-1980s second team.

Frank went into the construction business back in Lexington, starting up Minnifield All-Pro Homes upon retirement. He became the first African-American executive to be named to the executive board of the Lexington Chamber of Commerce. We still keep in constant contact to this day.

I Am Responsible for Donnie Rogers' Death

He was quiet, polite, demure. But oh, could he hit. Donnie Rogers was one of the biggest hitters I ever had the privilege of playing alongside. What a talented but troubled individual. The tragedy of his way-too-premature death haunts me to this day. Yes, Donnie was his own man and was responsible for his own actions. But the deeper tragedy behind this story is that I could have prevented it.

Donnie was born into poverty in Sacramento, California. But he was blessed with boyish good looks and tremendous athletic ability. His brother Reggie and sister Jackie were similarly gifted. They grew up with their mother Loretha in the Strawberry Hill section of northern Sacramento—a neighborhood tangled with streets of drugs and despair. But at Norte Del Rio High School, Donnie excelled on the field, on the court, and in the classroom. His wizardry on the football field and routine flying dunks on the basketball court brought him scholarship offers from many directions, and he wound up at UCLA. Donnie quickly made his mark as a devastating hitter and tight cover man. His freshman year, he was tutored by the great Kenny Easley, who went on to have a standout NFL career with the Seattle Seahawks.

In his sophomore year, Donnie stepped into the role of leader of the Bruins' defense. He set a school record with 133 tackles, breaking Easley's record. The Bruins went to the Rose Bowl, and

Donnie was named MVP. By the time his college career ended, the list of All-American honors was lengthy—Football Coaches' Poll, Football Writers' Poll, Walter Camp, *Playboy*, the *Sporting News*, *Football News*, *College and Pro Football Weekly*, Associated Press, United Press International, *Los Angeles Times* Player of the Year. Donnie was poised to enter the National Football League. The world was at his fingertips. Stardom, multimillion dollar contract, admiration, you name it.

He was the de facto head of the house and a light of hope to a beleaguered community. Donnie took all of the accolades quietly behind that glimmering broad smile. He was totally non-judgmental. Yet he yearned to be liked. By everyone. Remember that theme.

His style and technique fit right into what Coach Rutigliano wanted in Cleveland. With the 18th pick in the first round in the 1984 draft, the Browns selected the 6-foot-1 inch, 206-pound Bruin. He arrived in Cleveland the day after the draft and was greeted at the airport by Calvin Hill. The two had dinner together, and Calvin did his best to convince Donnie that the NFL was the place for him. The San Antonio Gunslingers of the USFL also drafted Donnie, then they traded his rights to the Arizona Wranglers, the same team from which the Browns wrangled Frank Minnifield that same year.

At the start of camp, Donnie showed the same awe and respect I had felt when I arrived three years earlier. He was quiet, paid attention, listened to what he was told, and carried out the usual rookie duties without a whisper of complaint. On the practice field, he lived up to his billing—bone-crushing tackles, gumming up running lanes, and staying step for step with our wide receivers with gazelle-like speed and style. Sam quickly named him the starting safety, and with me and Minnie shutting down the corners, we truly had the top defensive backfield in the NFL.

The 1984 season also was the same year the whole Dawg Pound saga began. At first, Donnie didn't quite know what to make of all of it. All of this barking seemed a bit silly to him at first since he was a quiet, easy-going guy. But he eventually caught on with the rest of us. We had two scrimmages against Buffalo, mostly for rookies and free agents, and lost them both. Our offense tended to self-destruct.

Keep that theme in mind as well.

The exhibition season was very unremarkable. We went 1-3, including a 31-14 blasting at the hands of those goddamn Steelers, and essentially got our asses kicked. Donnie, a bit jittery at the beginning but eventually his usual steely self, started and played most the game.

Some fans might remember that game as the one and only time we wore uniforms with orange numerals. The Browns had decided to abandon the orange pants that we wore from 1975 to '83, which was fine, but they stupidly redesigned the whole uniform. You would think the Browns would have known better than to mess with tradition. The jerseys had these big-ass, wide orange bars on the sleeves, and the fluorescent orange numbers made us look like a bunch of fucking radioactive clowns. No one liked them, and the resulting protest by the fans brought about a quick change. The Browns ordered 200 new jerseys at $30 apiece. The basic design stayed the same, but the orange numerals were gone. The club then went back to its more traditional look in 1985.

The lone win we had in the preseason was particularly sweet for Donnie, as we beat the Los Angeles Rams, 21-10, in L.A., where Donnie's family was able to see him take down four tackles and pick off a pass. Nonetheless, with the Dawg Pound now growing exponentially every week and still feeling the sting of just missing the playoffs in 1983, we were ready for a big year. Beat writers polled by *Football Digest* picked us to win the division. And it turned out to be a very big year, but not in the manner we had hoped.

Sam had two years left on his contract as head coach, and Art Modell was very public in his admiration of his coach, probably because they both spoke fluent Brooklynese. As training camp began, he told the media, "Sam is going to be here a long time," and that in the next few weeks, they would sit down over lunch and come up with a new contract "in 30 seconds." He already had given Sam two extensions since he took over head coaching duties in 1978, and Art now gave him an extension into 1988. Sam told a meeting of the Cleveland Touchdown Club, "It's not going to be a long year." Sam turned out to be too prophetic.

Week 1 of the regular season had us going to Seattle. We were ready, so we thought. But offensively we got nowhere fast, and we got blasted, 33-0. Week 2 took us to Los Angeles, and we had to deal with the strains of a second consecutive West Coast trip. Excuses aside, we relinquished a 17-10 fourth-quarter lead and lost to the Rams, 20-17, on a last-minute field goal. We opened our home schedule in Week 3 hosting the Denver Broncos and their hotshot quarterback and future Browns foil John Elway. After jumping on them, 14-0, two interceptions and a fumble later resulted in Broncos 24, Browns 14. This great season we were supposed to have was now fucking 0-3.

Losing football games in Cleveland is the fastest way to bumhood. The Browns hadn't won a world title since 1964, and the town was overdue. And this was supposed to have been the year. Still, Sam and Art weren't panicked. Paul McDonald was now on the hot seat. Despite being booed by the sellout crowd in Week 4 and throwing his third interception returned for a touchdown, Paul got it together and we knocked off the goddamn Steelers. Hope once again sprang eternal.

Any week we beat the Steelers, the city indulges in temporary vicarious world championship afterglow. But we were just four games into the season, and the heat was already beginning to build on Sam. The day after the win over the goddamn Steelers, a reporter asked Sam if he was a better coach this week than he was last week, and the usually gregarious Sam turned gruff.

"That's not true, and I know you're trying to be funny," Sam snapped back. "I was a good coach a week ago, and I was a good coach when I came here. I don't let anybody evaluate Sam Rutigliano. That doesn't mean a damn thing to me. I believe in myself, and there's an awful lot of other people that do also . . . in spite of people's opinions, as opposed to the facts."

But the trouble was just beginning. We lost the next four in a row. The next week in Kansas City, everyone contributed negatively to a 10-6 loss. Paul threw four interceptions, and several dropped balls, especially late in the game, sealed it. I blew an easy interception late in the first half, allowing the Chiefs to continue a scoring drive that tied the game.

In a game against the Patriots, we blew a 16-3 lead but rallied back. We were trailing, 17-16, and were sitting on the Pats' 21 with 23 seconds to go. Certainly within easy field goal distance. But Sam called for one more pass, an out pattern to Duriel Harris down by the 5-yard line. Duriel slipped, and Raymond Clayborn (whom the Browns would sign six years later), picked it off. Holy Red Right 88 Retro.

After we blew another fourth quarter lead to the Jets, followed by a 12-9 loss in Cincinnati, Sam was called to Art's home, nestled on 32 acres in Waite Hill, and was given the boot. I'm sure it must have devastated Sam, who had been named Coach of the Year in 1979 and 1980. He was a great coach, and is an even better man. But football is a business of winning and losing, and these blunders in the final weeks, among others earlier in the year, sealed his fate.

One glaring example was playing many of the regulars all the way in the final exhibition game, the third game in 11 days. "That might be to [the players'] advantage," Sam told the media. Result: Two starting linemen got hurt in the fourth quarter, one of them, future Pro Bowl tackle Cody Risien, was out for the year.

Marty Schottenheimer took over head coaching duties, but agreed to it only after Art gave him a contract through the 1986 season.

At our first team meeting after Marty was promoted, he told us we all had a role in Sam's professional demise, and we all shared in the blame. But it was now water under the bridge and time to move forward.

Sam was the one who had brought Donnie on board. He studied films along with Marty. The Browns did an extensive background search on Donnie's past and present. They knew all about him, his dimensions, his statistics. They talked to his coaches, trainers, assistant coaches, even relatives. They were not about to make a very expensive first-round mistake. The consensus was that Donnie was solid, quick, and clean. After he was drafted, he passed a drug screen. Nobody had anything bad to say about Donnie. He came to camp focused on being an impact player from the first day.

I took on Donnie like a little brother, just as Ozzie Newsome had done for me. Donnie was eager to learn and let his actions on the field do his talking. We stumbled to a 5-11 record in 1984, and despite our dismal record, we finished with the top defense in the league. Despite separating his shoulder in the middle of the season, Donnie made 105 tackles and was Defensive Rookie of the Year. We had a good off-season, and I kept in touch with Frank and Donnie. We talked about everything and everyone, determined that 1985 was going to be the big year. After the Browns unsuccessfully attempted to pick up Doug Flutie, and thanks to some clever draft-posturing techniques, Bernie Kosar positioned himself to be picked up by the Browns in the 1985 supplemental draft. The big, lanky kid from Boardman, Ohio, just 65 miles or so southeast of Cleveland, brought a new excitement to the offensive side of the ball.

But it was becoming evident that Donnie's unfounded insecurities were leading him down the wrong path. On any given team, there are a group of good guys, a group of bad guys, and a group of followers. It's easy to be liked by the good guys. But Donnie wanted to be liked by all the guys, including the ones he should have stayed clear of. I suspected Donnie was surfing too closely to the drug culture, but still, he was his own man. I never saw him touch drugs, and he never said anything to me about doing drugs. But the circumstantial evidence was becoming more clear. Sam mentioned in his book *Pressure* that there was something different about Donnie.

"I discovered that Donnie Rogers was a follower," Sam wrote. "He desperately wanted to be accepted by his peers. A football team has a small group of negative people and small group of positive ones. Donnie began to follow the negative ones. It was his choice. I wasn't the only one who saw that he wasn't keeping the best of company."

*   *   *

The 1985 season was a fun year. I signed a new contract for $250,000. Frank, Donnie, and I had the Dawg Pound cranking every week. The Browns brought in veteran quarterback Gary Danielson, the plan being that Bernie would sit at his knee for the first year or two and learn from Gary's experience. But in Week 5, Gary went down with an injury, and Bernie the Kid was handed the keys. Despite fumbling his first snap, Bernie went on to complete his first seven passes and led us to a 24-20 win over New England. Donnie made some huge stops in the fourth quarter to seal the win.

Kevin Mack and Earnest Byner both had 1,000-yard seasons. Ozzie caught 62 passes. Despite the flashy numbers, we actually stumbled our way through the season and finished 8-8. Four of the losses were by a touchdown or less. We became the first team in NFL history to win a division with a .500 record. We played in Miami in the first round, where Frank and I had our infamous bathtub blowup the night before. We built a 21-3 third-quarter lead on big touchdown rips by Mack and Byner, and Donnie had a huge goal-line interception of Dan Marino that he almost took all the way back. But Marino and Tony Nathan took advantage of the fact that Eddie Johnson was playing out of position and worked their way back to a 24-21 win. I saw a most unbelievable sight when Nathan scored the winning touchdown—he ran over Donnie. That just never happened to Donnie.

But life was looking good for the Browns. I was at the peak of my career, and the Browns were about to enter one of the most exciting eras of the franchise. Donnie had a breakout season, leading the team with 154 tackles. Except for Kenny Easley and Donnie, it was rare for a safety to lead the team in tackles. If your safety leads the team in tackles, either he's a helluva player or your linebackers suck. But with Clay Matthews, Eddie Johnson and Chip Banks at linebacker, we were solid there. Donnie was just so quick and read the plays so well, it was like he was playing safety and doubling as a fourth linebacker at the same time. Donnie was now two years into his three-year contract, and unless he tanked his third year, he stood to sign a deal that would take care of him and his family for the rest of their lives.

And Donnie had more good news—he was getting married to Leslie Nelson in June. Donnie was already the father of 3-year-old Donnie Jr., and now this was going to complete the family picture. He asked me to be one of the ushers. Kenny Easley was the best man, and Donnie's brother Reggie, another promising star (and another subsequent tragedy), was also to be an usher. The date was set for June 28, 1986, in a spectacular wedding in Oakland officiated by her father.

About a week before the wedding, I casually flipped on the television and was greeted by shocking news from Maryland. Len Bias, the great All-America forward for the Terrapins who had just been drafted by the Boston Celtics with the second overall pick in 1986, had just died from a cocaine overdose. Len was another guy who had the world in the palm of his hand. He was already being favorably compared to Michael Jordan, who had just finished his second year. But the instant fame came at an incendiary and fatal cost. Before the ink was dry on his $3 million endorsement contract with Reebok, Bias was just another lumpy body bag in the morgue. An absolute fucking waste of a world-class talent. But no one foresaw anything about how this could somehow happen in the Browns' world.

I flew from Cleveland to Sacramento two days before the wedding. I was picked up by limo and taken to the Hilton. Donnie purposely wanted a low-key bachelor party, and that was the evening fare. We were all laid back and having a good time, and then Donnie called me over. "Hanford," he said. "I want you to ride with me to Oakland tomorrow for the wedding rehearsal. There's something important I want to tell you."

"Sure," I responded, not quite sure what he had in mind for the 90-mile trip. We had a suite on the top floor of the Hilton, and we spent that evening just chillin' and eating. No big deal, no big, wild, intoxicating drink-a-thon. There were a few teammates from the Browns, the UCLA Bruins, and some childhood friends. After a while, Donnie excused himself and headed for the door. He had a woman on each arm. I could tell by the look in his eye that this was trouble. Not just the fact that here he is about to be married and he's walking out with a woman on each arm. I knew what he was going to do. I just knew it. It was going to be his last hurrah. His last great party. I'm sure to this day that he wanted to get the whole drug thing over with, and that's what he was going to tell me the next day on the way to Oakland. He walked past me, and I looked in his eyes. I knew what was going to happen.

*   *   *

There is an unwritten code among entertainers and athletes: We leave each other be. We didn't get into each other's business. Donnie was his own man, capable of making his own decisions. As a subscriber to the code, I told Donnie to have a good time, and he departed. But now I realize why I was there. I loved Donnie like a little brother. And big brothers have responsibilities. Damn the code. I should have stood up and spun Donnie by the arm, looked him in the eye, and said "No fucking way, brother. You're not going to do this to yourself." But I was too beholden to the code. Like a typical wimpy teenager, I was concerned about what others might think of me.

But I know God put me there in that place and that time to stop this tragedy. All I had to do was be a real man right then, right there. So what if someone turned out not to like me? Hell with them. If I knew some punkass was going to hand one of my kids some drugs, my fist would be through his face faster than he could think. And if someone ever did give drugs to my kids and there was someone there who could have prevented it, I could only imagine how long and hard I would be in his face screaming "Why didn't you stop it?" Donnie was Loretha's son and my little brother. I blew the biggest chance I had to be a true man. In this sense, I feel I am responsible for Donnie Rogers' death. I didn't give him the drugs, I never said, "Go do it." But I wimped out, and the result was the same. All these years later, no one has ever criticized me for upholding the god-damn code. But I'm sure everyone who knew Donnie wishes I had violated it. Especially his mother. God, how could I ever look her in the eye?

Late Friday morning, the day before the wedding, I woke to a loud fist pounding that sounded like it was going to break through the door. "What the fuck?" I muttered to myself, not wanting to open the door. I figured some of the guys from the party were still up and drunk and wanted to fuck around, and I was in no such mood. But the pounding continued, and I heard Reggie yell out "Hanford, get up!" I opened the door, and Reggie blurted out in a panic, "They took Donnie to the hospital. They took Donnie to the hospital."

"Quit shittin' me," I said, waiting for the relieving punch line that never came. Reggie was serious. A few of us scrambled to put ourselves together, jammed ourselves in a car, and raced to the two-story home Donnie had bought for his mother in the South Natomas development two years earlier.

About 20 minutes later, we arrived at Loretha's house, where Christmas lights still hung on the outside. We all sat around in stunned silence. The minutes dragged on for hours. We heard Donnie had been taken to nearby Community Hospital and was subsequently transferred to the larger Mercy San Juan Hospital. Just after

4:30 that afternoon, the phone rang. I don't know who answered it, but the conversation was short.

"Donnie's gone."

Twenty-fucking-three years old. Shit.

Waves of emotion washed through the house like a tsunami. Disbelief. Anger. Tears. The magnitude of this tragedy was just beginning. It didn't take long for me to realize that this was quickly going to turn into a media circus and police dragnet. I wanted no part of either. I called my agent and attorney, Bud Holmes.

"Get your things and get out of there," he told me. "Nothing good can come of you hanging around there."

I made a second call, this time to Art Modell. I told him briefly what had happened and that I was coming back to Cleveland. This was of course in the pre-cellphone era, so it took a while for all of the subsequent calls to the right people for the news to propagate its way through. Marty was at his kid's baseball game in Strongsville, and Browns public relations director Kevin Byrne found him in the stands and delivered the horrific news. Marty broke down.

I got a ride to the airport, went to the ticket counter. "Give me the first flight to Cleveland," I stammered, not caring what the cost or number of connections. I would have to wait two hours, which seemed more like 10. I sat down at a bar and had a couple drinks to calm my nerves. But all this crazy shit kept going through my head. I couldn't help but feel responsible. I was the safety. I blew the assignment. I kept looking over my shoulder for law enforcement personnel and the strobe-like flash bulbs of the hyper-questioning media. I had nothing to hide, but this was one of the worst days in my life, and the last thing I wanted to do was give an account to anyone, especially since I really had no idea what had just transpired.

Once back in Cleveland, I retreated to my apartment. I talked to a few teammates and to Kevin Byrne. I told him I didn't want to make any public statements, but Kevin told me I should say something. He helped put together a brief statement for me which didn't say a whole lot, mainly because I really didn't know a whole lot.

While dealing with the shock and grief was bad enough for me, what was about to happen to the Rogers family was exponentially worse. His family didn't believe, or at least didn't want to believe or publicly admit, that drugs could be involved. Donnie's agent, Steve Arnold, told the Associated Press that he would be "totally surprised if there was any drug involvement. Chances are 99-1 against any drug connection." Art Modell said he would be "very, very surprised and upset" if drugs were found to be involved. But the preliminary autopsy report showed there was no evidence of physical disease or deformity, which left only one likely cause—drugs. Cocaine, specifically. I already knew that, sadly, but didn't want to say anything to Loretha. When the news of the preliminary autopsy broke, it was too much for Loretha to take. She collapsed into Reggie's arms, stricken by unimaginable heartbreak and now a heart attack. When the final toxicology report came in, it was found that Donnie had five times the fatal dose of cocaine in his system.

I returned to Sacramento a few days later for the funeral. There were two funerals that day, the one in California and one at the Old Stone Church in downtown Cleveland. I felt I had to go to the one in Sacramento to be with the family. I wanted to pay my respects to his mother, but she was still in the hospital. Eddie Johnson, Frank Minnifield, Curtis Weathers, Al Gross, and Webster Slaughter were there as well. I was a pallbearer, along with Donnie's UCLA teammates Kenny Easley, Frank Cephous, Gene Mewborn, and Kevin Nelson. Altogether, there were about 5,000 people attending the open-casket service at ARCO Arena.

As sad as the whole scene was, the real depth of the tragedy was thrust upon the most innocent. Donnie's 4-year-old son, Donnie Jr., also known as "Little D," didn't know what was going on. Amid the grief and chaos in the hours after his father's death, no one had sat down and explained to him what happened. When the limo arrived at the arena, Little D became excited, thinking they were all going to a Sacramento Kings game. The family filed onto the arena floor, and instead of seeing LaSalle Thompson or Mike Woodson or Otis Thorpe, Little D saw his daddy lying motionless in a box. Cruel reality instantly ripped away the precious boy's innocence.

Reverend Jesse Jackson spoke at the service and railed against drug pushers. "The KKK, as the shadow of death, and the rope, has never killed as many young people as the pushers of dope. Pushers are terrorists and death messengers," he preached in his familiar syncopated style. Just a few days earlier, Rev. Jackson had eulogized Len Bias, saying, "On a day the children mourn, I hope they learn." Certainly one cannot argue with what Rev. Jackson said, but drugs weren't pushed on Donnie. He sought them out. If there were no demand, the pushers would be out of business. We didn't learn enough from the death of Len Bias, nor from the drug-induced death of comedian John Belushi in 1982, or that of Elvis Presley in 1977, or Janis Joplin or Jimi Hendrix in 1970, and, most tragically, we still haven't learned enough from Donnie's horrid loss. Or from Chris Farley, Michael Jackson, Amy Winehouse, Ike Turner, and Whitney Houston, just to name a few.

Former *Washington Post* columnist Michael Wilbon aptly noted, "If Don Rogers . . . could die a similar death as Len Bias' just eight days later, you have to wonder how many people said, as Bias did, 'Well, it won't happen to me.' "

After the service, we carefully loaded our brother into the hearse for the short ride to the Chapel of the Chimes, a cemetery in North Sacramento. Goddammit, I was supposed to be in California working as an usher in his wedding, not a pallbearer for this fucking funeral.

Loretha recovered from the heart attack but died in 2000 of heart failure. Reggie was drafted by the Detroit Lions with the seventh overall pick in 1987 but never realized his potential. While he managed to stay away from drugs, alcohol was his downfall. In October 1988, Reggie was involved in a fatal crash that took the lives of three teenagers. He was sentenced to 16 months in prison. Reggie tried to make a comeback with Buffalo and then Tampa Bay, but injuries (he broke his neck in the accident) and his constant struggle with alcohol led to him being tagged as one of the biggest draft busts in league history. His sister Jackie, a promising star on the basketball court at Oregon State, slipped into the clutches of drugs like her brother.

*   *   *

I'm often asked if the Browns had a drug problem. The fact is that the Browns were typical of any other professional sports franchise. The Browns were not unique in having a drug problem, nor was the drug problem any better or worse with the Browns compared to any other professional sports franchise. Get a group of ambitious twenty-something guys, throw a few million dollars at them, and line up scores of admiring fans, plunging-neckline women, and others who want a piece of the lifestyle and surreptitious access to the cash. What could possibly go wrong there?

Unlike most other teams, the Browns took very public steps to deal with this issue. Sam formed the Inner Circle, similar in format to Alcoholics Anonymous. This program was in effect before Donnie's tragedy. Art fully funded the program, where anyone with a problem could privately get treatment, both in support and medically. Some of the guys in the program entered it voluntarily; others were told they had better get involved or their football careers were over. I know the Inner Circle did help many—mostly those who truly wanted to overcome their problem. And no, I am not going to reveal any names of those who were in the program, only to say that I was not ever involved in it. Donnie was not involved in it, although he did attend one meeting. The only person who publicly admitted his participation was Charles White. That's not to say I never experimented with anything, because there were some times through college and beyond that I tried marijuana. That puts me in the ranks with about 90 percent of the population.

Not only was the membership of the Inner Circle kept quiet,

the program itself was kept quiet at first. The July 25, 1983, issue of *Newsweek* magazine, in an article by contributing editor Pete Axthelm, revealed its existence. The group met every Monday with Sam, former players, and front office guys Calvin Hill and Paul Warfield, Dr. Greg Collins, and Tom Petersburg. Dr. Collins was a psychiatrist who specialized in chemical dependency, and Tom led our twice-weekly chapel services as well as being a counselor for the Fellowship of Christian Athletes. They also would meet with a chapter of Narcotics Anonymous and once a week with Dr. Collins at the Cleveland Clinic. Eight players formed the group, and to stay in it, they had to pass a drug test twice a week. If they failed, they would be cut or traded. NFL Commissioner Pete Rozelle cited the Inner Circle as a way that teams were effectively dealing with the growing drug problem in the league.

The *New York Daily News* ran a five-part series detailing the drug problem in the NFL, claiming 20 percent of the players were "hooked" on cocaine and about 50 percent were, or had been, "casual users." Sam thought that number was outrageous.

Well, if eight players on the Browns were in rehab, that constitutes about 16 percent. Not too far from the 20 percent figure the *Daily News* contended. And I can tell you from first-hand knowledge that the *Daily News* was pretty close. Just before the 1986 draft, the league tested 350 prospects for drug use, and 57 of them, or 16 percent, had traces of marijuana or cocaine in their systems.

Sam originally started a "chain of support" in 1981 to help players who had drug problems, but that didn't go very far. Despite this, Sam took this issue very seriously, and decided to push forward with the more comprehensive Inner Circle program instead of just filing things away and thinking the availability of help through the "chain of support" relieved him of any further moral obligation. Sam's emphasis was on help and treatment for these guys, not punishment.

"You don't cure a case of dandruff by using a guillotine," Sam said at a July 20, 1983, news conference where he gave details, but no names of participants, of the program. "That's only driving people deeper into the woods. What we are talking about is the possibility of saving a guy's life."

*   *   *

Despite a criminal investigation by the Sacramento Police, who did interview me, no one was ever prosecuted in Donnie's death. In the 2007 book *One Moment Changes Everything*, author Sean D. Harvey strongly suggests that Terry Bolar, an aspiring agent at the time, was the likely source of the drugs that took Donnie's life. But Donnie was well known by all too many people, so if Donnie wanted drugs, he certainly had his own contacts.

Sam got into some trouble with Art a couple of months later when he told the *Sacramento Bee*, "Now that Donnie is gone, everyone's an ostrich," and that the drug problem with the Browns had worsened since his departure because Marty wasn't as deeply involved with the Inner Circle as he was. Sam contended that since Donnie had tested clean before he was drafted, he must have been introduced to drugs by his teammates. This enraged Marty and Art, who threatened possible legal action against Sam. Sam clarified his comments a few days later, stating that while he believed Donnie was introduced to drugs after he joined the Browns, he wasn't accusing anyone of the team of being the culprit, and Art and Marty had "overreacted" to his comments.

*   *   *

The twin tragedies of Donnie Rogers and Len Bias led to numerous changes in drug laws and plenty of politicians climbing over each other to demand action the loudest. Some changes and awareness-raising were laudable, others were just screwball. U.S. Congresswoman Maxine Waters of Los Angeles even went so far as to promote the idea that crack had been introduced into America by the Central Intelligence Agency as a method of exterminating the black race. Only a few years earlier, some idiots (many of the same crowd) contended that AIDS had been introduced into America the same way for the same reason.

On October 27, 1986, Congress passed the sweeping Anti Drug-Abuse Act. I don't know all of the particulars of that law, but then again, the politicians who passed it didn't know much about it either. Then Representative Trent Lott of Mississippi said, "In our haste to patch together a drug bill—any drug bill—before Congress adjourns, we have run the risk of ending up with a patchwork quilt that may not fit together into a comprehensive whole." Nine years after that law was passed, the prison population had doubled. I don't know whether that's a good thing or bad, just so very sad.

But why all the scrutiny on professional athletes? I think Calvin Hill, writing for *Browns News/Illustrated*, put it best when he wrote, "Where was the indignation when Elvis (Presley) died? Why is there no sentiment to pass the bottle to rock groups before they perform at the Coliseum? Why is there no sentiment for every entertainer to be tested before he or she appears on television? There are lots of people whose job performance directly affects others— bus drivers, airline pilots, doctors, dentists, politicians, policemen. Are we as a society more concerned about an athlete who carries a football than a policeman who carries a gun?"

Indiana University men's basketball coach Bobby Knight, never short of sharp opinions, said of the tragedy, "It's time to go to war. We're fighting an insidious monster. It's time we stopped chasing the drug boats; it's time we started sinking them."

*   *   *

Soon after Donnie's burial, Art made it clear that the Browns were going to get tough on personal conduct issues in the organization. From the steps of the Old Stone Church downtown, right after Donnie's memorial service, Art proclaimed, "We will get tough. We are not going to tolerate off-season indiscretions." Twice in

June, the same month Donnie died, defensive end Sam Clancy was arrested for driving while intoxicated. The Browns cut Willie Smith, a 10th-round draft pick that year, for possession of cocaine and a gun. He was arrested three days after Donnie's death.

The Browns never offered any type of tribute to Donnie in the year following his death. Often when a prominent team member or administrative figure, past or present, dies, the team wears a patch or emblem in tribute. Ernie Davis was a Heisman Trophy-winning running back from Syracuse whom the Browns acquired in a trade after being drafted with the first overall pick in 1962 by the Washington Redskins. He died of leukemia a year later before he ever played a down. The Browns retired his number 45. Don Fleming was an all-pro defensive back for the Browns, drafted in the 28th round in 1959. The afternoon after the Browns announced Don had signed a contract extension, he was fatally electrocuted in a construction accident in Florida—17 days after Ernie died. The Browns retired his number 46.

But the Browns wanted nothing of the sort with Donnie. They did put a picture of Donnie in the lunchroom, but that was it. I'm not saying Donnie's number should be retired or anything like that, and yes, Don and Ernie didn't self-destruct like Donnie did. But something more should have been done for Donnie, for the good things he did for others far outweighed the bad thing he did to himself.

I believe that had this horrible tragedy not taken place, the Browns would have won at least two Super Bowls. This is a game of inches, and we needed only one or two plays where Donnie's incredible athletic ability would have made the difference. But more important, Leslie would have a husband, Loretha would have a son, Reggie would have a big brother and little Donnie would have a caring father. If only I'd had the balls to violate the code. If I had just said no.

CHAPTER NINE

Favorite Game #2: Browns vs. Steelers, Oct. 5, 1986

We had tried everything to beat the Three Rivers jinx. We stayed at different hotels. In 1985, we brought dirt from Cleveland Stadium and spread it around the field at Three Rivers Stadium. This year we flew to Pittsburgh instead of taking the three-hour bus ride. We had come so close so many times.

In 1984, I intercepted two passes in this stadium, but we still lost, 23-20, as Gary Anderson kicked a game winner with five seconds left.

In 1985, Matt Bahr hit a 30-yard field goal with just over four minutes left to put us up, 9-7, but we couldn't hold them on defensive as the goddamn Steelers drove 73 yards on us, making a hero out of Anderson again as he kicked the game winner through a driving rain with nine seconds left.

In my rookie year, we were trailing, 13-7, but driving for the winning score when a pass from Paul McDonald to Ozzie Newsome got tipped and then intercepted in the end zone by J.T. Thomas with just under two minutes to go.

The Browns were 0-16 in Three Rivers Stadium, with 12 of those 16 losses coming in the final two minutes or in overtime. Seven games of the previous nine in Three Rivers were lost by six points or fewer. The goddamn Steelers had won 99 games in their shitty cereal-bowl stadium since it was built in 1970, and this was their 112th home sellout.

In 1978, three years before I arrived, the Browns got hosed in Three Rivers. The Steelers' Larry Anderson clearly fumbled the overtime kickoff deep in Pittsburgh territory, and Ricky Feacher came up with it, but the refs said the whistle had blown the play dead. Clearly, that must have been the world's fastest whistle. Instant replay was still eight years away, but it wouldn't have made any difference since a whistle kills the play no matter what. The goddamn Steelers then drove on, converting on a fourth-and-1 at midfield, then pulling some backyard juvenile jack-shit double reverse-flea flicker pass from Bradshaw to Bennie Cunningham for the winning score.

In 1979, the Browns lost in the final seconds of overtime, 33-30, in a game that Brian Sipe played not long after his father died. Talk about unbelievable heart and concentration.

But this was going to be the year. We knew it. We were a better team, and the goddamn Steelers were regressing. I had decided after Donnie Rogers' death that I was going to be different. I stopped all the yipping and yapping at opposing wide receivers. I declined most locker-room interviews. I was going to let my actions do the talking.

We were 2-2 going into the game. We had lost to the world champion Bears on opening day, then beat the Oilers in Week 2. I began chattering again that week, and did all I could to get into rookie Ernest Givins' head. It worked. From my film study, I was able to read what pattern he was going to run based on how he lined up. I snagged an easy interception as a result. We then lost to the Bengals and beat the Lions.

The goddamn Steelers were 1-3 and had been wracked by injuries, and their quarterback, Mark Malone, was statistically the worst quarterback in the league, toting a 31.6 passer rating. They were going to be without receiver John Stallworth and running back Walter

Abercrombie, and defensive backs Eric Williams, Rick Woods, and Chris Sheffield were hurting. In the three games that the goddamn Steelers lost, they were ripped through the air. In fact, the injury situation for the goddamn Steelers was so bad, coach Chuck Noll improvised a 3-5-3 defense at times.

We had some key injuries as well. Kevin Mack was out with a sore shoulder, and Ozzie Newsome had a gimpy ankle. Gary Danielson broke and dislocated his ankle in the last exhibition game, a preseason that saw us go 4-0. Sports talker Pete Franklin of WWWE radio said he would single-handedly end the curse by attending the game dressed in a babushka. For two weeks, he played a rap parody, "Beat the Jinx," written by his producer, Dave Dombrowski, and sung by the Pigskin Pete Rappers.

Yet the local media tried to downplay the significance of the game while playing up the goddamn Steelers' situation. *The Plain Dealer's* Bob Dolgan wrote a column that had the headline, "Noll has proven he's an outstanding coach." *PD* writer Tony Grossi's story had a headline that gleefully reminded us that the "Browns certainly aren't offensive." Another Grossi column pitied Mark Malone, calling him the "Maligned Steeler." The headline on Bill Livingston's column proclaimed the "AFC Central is a sad bunch."

"Let's spare the talk about the 'Three Rivers Jinx' this week," Livingston wrote. "That angle is as weak as the two teams who will play there." Certainly one couldn't accuse the print media in Cleveland as being homers.

But in the Sunday *Plain Dealer*, I boldly predicted to Grossi that "The game will be decided on a big play." Grossi went on to say that if indeed there was going to be a decisive big play, it would be pulled off by either Clay Matthews, Chips Banks, me, or Gerald McNeil. Chip, along with Eddie Johnson, had held out for a while during training camp. In fact, Chip at one time wanted a guarantee that he would play on third down.

One hot day during Gerald's first camp, he was having lunch with punter Jeff Gossett. Jeff noticed an ice cube on his lunch tray and tried to pick it up. The little ice cube kept squirting away. It was slippery, elusive, and small. As the antithesis to William "The Refrigerator" Perry of the Chicago Bears, Jeff came up with the perfect name for Gerald McNeil: "The Ice Cube."

The Browns listed The Cube as weighing in at 140 pounds. Like hell. Try more like 125. In camp, the staff mistook him for a ball boy.

The Browns acquired the Ice Cube in the second round of the 1984 supplemental draft. Prior to that, the Cube played for the Houston Gamblers of the United States Football League. He set several reception records at Baylor University. He was a little guy with a huge heart. In the previous week's game at home against Detroit, the Cube returned a punt for a club-record 84 yards for a touchdown in a 24-21 win.

The Cube told Grossi in that same article that he goes into every game thinking "of one big play because it can be the difference in a close game. I can see it now: fourth quarter . . . two minutes to go . . . and I bust one. I'd love it."

It was a crisp and clear early October day in Pittsburgh. We went through our usual routines and preparations, trying to put aside any more thought about this stupid jinx. We knew that if we played our game, today would be the day. We were sharp and focused in practice all week. Ozzie kept reminding us about what a great week we had. Marty Schottenheimer kept telling us all week that "this was going to be our Sunday." He was right. We were ready.

The goddamn Steelers took the opening kickoff but missed a 43-yard field goal wide right. On our first possession, Bernie's first pass, intended for Herman Fontenot, was intercepted, but an offside penalty against the goddamn Steelers negated the play. We marched ahead, but Matt Bahr missed from 50. The goddamn Steelers got the ball back, and Frank Minnifield looked like he had hurt his knee. Spotting this, the goddamn Steelers decided to go after him. Louis Lipps, a fellow University of Southern Mississippi product, raced down the seam, but Frank out-leapt him for the interception.

Bernie countered by launching a deep throw for Webster

Slaughter, but Harvey Clayton grabbed Webster to prevent what would have been an easy score. The result was a 53-yard penalty. Three plays later, Bernie hit Webster for a 15-yard score, and Slaughter punctuated his first NFL touchdown with an extra hard spike. Then another big play on the kickoff. Travis Tucker forced a fumble, and Fontenot recovered on the Steelers' 22. We stalled on offense, but Matt's short field goal gave us a 10-0 lead and plenty of momentum. We would need it.

Later on, The Cube dropped a pass that was a sure 80-yard score, and three plays later, Bernie fumbled the ball away at our own 10. It sure looked like Bernie's arm was in motion and thus should have been an incomplete pass, but the play withstood instant replay analysis. Malone scored from the 1 on third down. On the next series, Reggie Langhorne lost the ball after a 7-yard catch, and the Malone hit Rich Erenberg on a 5-yard touchdown pass, and just like that, our 10-point lead became a four-point deficit. What had been going so well for us was now taking an ugly and all-too-familiar turn.

On our sideline, The Cube got a face-full from Browns special teams coach—and future Steelers head coach—Bill Cowher. Amid the flying spittle and high-decibel provocative words, Bill, who played linebacker for us in his playing days before becoming special teams coach in 1985, yelled, "I'm sending you back out there. We're relying on you. We're going to win this game. Do you hear me?"

On the next kickoff, The Cube fielded the ball at the goal line and started upfield. He cut to the left side, took advantage of key blocks by Ralph Malone, Scott Nicolas, and Dave Puzzuoli, and it was over. The Cube sprinted down the left side for a 100-yard score with no one even mussing his hair, giving us back the lead and momentum just before halftime. It was the third-longest touchdown in Browns history and the team's first kickoff return for a score in 12 years. Greg Pruitt was the most recent Brown to return a kick 100 yards, accomplishing that in 1974.

While a halftime lead is certainly something you want, we knew that this game was far from over. There would be plenty of second-half drama. We had plenty of opportunities over the years to break the curse, only to let it get the best of us at the end. But Marty reminded us that "It's still our Sunday."

In the third quarter, The Cube fumbled a punt, and the goddamn Steelers took advantage. Malone faded back and tried to go to Calvin Sweeney in front of me, but I had him covered tight. So he instead looked over to Lipps and hit him for the 6-yard, go-ahead score. That was three scores converted off three turnovers. You can't give up scores off turnovers and expect to win the game. We ground out a 46-yard drive on the ground with Earnest Byner picking up 29 big yards on a draw, setting up a 39-yard field goal by Matt. But then Earnest Jackson ripped a 25-yard run to set up a 45-yard field goal by Anderson. The goddamn Steelers were now up, 24-20, their meager 57,000 fans were back in the game, and our offensive tackle, Paul Farren, went down with an injury. We would have to climb uphill in the fourth quarter.

Then another big play on special teams. Mike Johnson stripped the ball from Rick Woods on a punt, and Mark Harper recovered it at the Pittsburgh 34. Again the offense stalled, but was given new life when Dave Edwards ran into Matt as he missed a 43-yard field goal. Bernie then hit big passes to Brian Brennan and Earnest Byner, and Earnest then took it in from 4 yards out to give us the lead, 27-24.

But there were still eight minutes left, an eternity in Browns-Steelers legend.

With about four minutes left, we were camped near the Pittsburgh goal line, looking to deliver a knockout punch. But again we stalled, and Matt went out to kick a 24-yard chipper to at least make the goddamn Steelers have to score a touchdown to beat us. Inside 40 yards, Matt was as automatic as you could get. He had hit 40 in a row, dating back to 1982. No problem, right? Wrong. He missed it, and the goddamn Steelers still had life.

Pittsburgh came driving along. I got twisted around on Sweeney, and he beat me for a 23-yard gain. That was only the second completion to a wide receiver for Pittsburgh that afternoon.

Then on what was certainly one of the most bizarre calls of the year, Malone reversed out and headed left on an option play. Sam Clancy got to him and knocked the ball away. Earnest Jackson got a hold of it, but Clay Matthews knocked it away from him. Chris Rockins finally recovered it for us at the 29.

But there was still a fair amount of time left, and we were going to need at least one first down. Bernie hit Reggie for a 38-yard gainer, with Reggie having the presence of mind to run to the middle of the field instead of down the sideline where he might get pushed out. All that was left was three kneel-downs to drive the stake into the curse. As the clock reached triple zero, Bernie stole the ball and ran off the field. We had done it. The Three Rivers Jinx was over. Dead. And the goddamn Steelers were off to their worst start in 15 years. Delicious. Nothing could faze us now. It was indeed going to be a very special year. We went on to win 13 games that year, the most in franchise history. Livingston was full of crap.

Fresh out of the University of Southern Mississippi, I was ready to take on the world. *Cleveland Press Collection, Cleveland State University Archives*

Above: I share a moment with Johnny Davis after I picked off Terry Bradshaw three times as we beat the Steelers 10-9 in December 1982. *Akron Beacon Journal*

Left: At rookie mini-camp in 1981, I looked for opportunity. I was assigned number 40 at random. I wanted my old college number, 19, but couldn't have it. *Cleveland Press Collection, Cleveland State University Archives*

Above: Don Rogers, my little brother, at training camp in 1984. Had he not died from that cocaine overdose in 1987, I'm sure we would have won at least two Super Bowls. *Debra Foster Biagetti*

Right, top: After Keith Baldwin tipped the ball, I picked this pass off Warren Moon in 1984, setting up a touchdown in a victory over Houston. *The Plain Dealer /Landov*

Right, bottom: The Dawg Pound, born in 1984. Frank and I started the whole dawg thing. The fans made it their own.
Diamond Images

Above: With Frank before a game with the Oilers in Houston.
Diamond Images

Right: Frank Minnifield, Al Gross, and I talk
strategy during a break. *Diamond Images*

Above: Just for kicks one day Frank and I decided to strut out in fur coats before a game at the Stadium in 1986. *Melvin Grier*

Left: Walking off the field after we pounded the San Diego Chargers 47-17 in what was a "meaningless" game in 1986. We had wrapped up homefield for the playoffs, and went 12-4 in the regular season, a club record for wins. *Akron Beacon Journal*

Above: Frank, Clay Matthews, and I enjoy some sunshine and good company before the Pro Bowl. *Courtesy of Ray Yannucci*

Left: Keeping my feet warm during a playoff game against the Indianapolis Colts at the Stadium January 9, 1988. Much as I enjoyed the Pro Bowl in Hawaii, I loved playing home games in January even more. *Ron Kuntz Collection/Diamond Images*

Above: I was known for giving the refs a bit of a hard time. Here, in a game against the Bengals in December, 1989, they are obviously getting me steamed again. *The Plain Dealer / Landov*

Right: Nothing is sweeter than knocking off the Steelers at Three Rivers Stadium in the 1989 season opener. Six fumble recoveries and three defensive touchdowns paved the way. We held the Steelers to 53 net yards. *The News-Herald*

Above: Shortly after we both retired, I try to bring Walter Payton down one more time. *Author's collection.*

Right: The fans fed off me, and I fed off the fans, especially for those cold but memorable playoff games on the lakefront. These guys knew who the Top Dawgs were! *Tony Tomsic*

My favorite activity still is interacting with the fans. I just love it when a dad comes up to me and says to his 7-year-old son, "This is Hanford Dixon. He's the guy who started the Dawg Pound." Signing an autograph for a kid is at least as big of a thrill for me as it is for that kid. *Eleanore Lowery*

CHAPTER TEN

Favorite Game #3: Browns vs. Jets, Jan. 3, 1987

We were two teams streaking in opposite directions. In 1986, we won our last five games, giving us a franchise-record 12 wins in the regular season. We beat Cincinnati and San Diego, our last two opponents, by a combined score of 81-20. We allowed only seven sacks over those last five games. The Jets, on the other hand, had lost their last five regular-season games after bursting out to a 10-1 start, becoming the first NFL team to make the playoffs despite losing its last five games.

The New York media was doing a number on the Jets, and there were suggestions that quarterback Ken O'Brien should be benched. The Jets were the only playoff team to allow more points than it scored. They were also the most-penalized team in the league and gave up 27 touchdowns in their last six games. Meanwhile, we, the team that featured the youngest starting quarterback (Bernie) and the smallest kick returner (Gerald McNeil, 142 pounds) were enjoying one of the greatest love affairs between a city and a sports franchise.

While we enjoyed a week off, the Jets pitted their 28th-ranked pass defense against Kansas City's 28th-ranked offense. The Jets started nine-year veteran backup quarterback Pat Ryan, known to his teammates as "Mr. Guts," and, maximizing on their short passing attack, cruised to a 35-15 win. We spent the week before the game in Vero Beach, Florida, where we could concentrate on practicing and not worry about the weather. It made sense to have these practices in warm weather because it's next to impossible to install and practice a game plan if there's a foot of snow on the practice field, something that could strike at a moment's notice in Cleveland seven months out of the year.

This was going to be our first home playoff game since Red Right 88 ended the Kardiac Kids' season of 1980. The most recent time that the Browns had won a playoff game at home was when Bill Nelsen and crew led the Browns to a 38-14 win over the Cowboys. That was before the NFL-AFL merger. The city was going nuts. We were a touchdown favorite to beat the Jets and advance to the AFC title game, which we would host no matter who the opponent would be. On the NBC pregame show, Dolphins coach Don Shula, who played for the Browns during their glory days of the 1950s, picked us to win, saying he was very impressed with how we won three weeks before against "Cincinnada." That's how he pronounced it—"Cincinnada." Play-by-play man Don Criqui noted, "I've never been in a louder, more exuberant crowd at the outset of this game."

We knew we couldn't take the Jets lightly. The previous year, we played them in the final regular-season game and got thrashed, 37-10, after jumping out to a 10-0 lead. The Jets' offense revolved around running back Freeman McNeil, who was drafted out of UCLA 20 picks ahead of me in 1981. He picked up only 856 yards on the ground in 1986, a bit of a contrast to the career-high 1,331 he gained in 1985. A three time Pro-Bowler, McNeil was part of the "two-headed monster" backfield the Jets featured in the mid-'80s along with running back Johnny Hector. McNeil is one of the few players to average at least 4.0 yards per carry each season he played, especially impressive since his career spanned 12 years.

In the NBC pregame show, analyst Paul Maguire noted that as far as the Jets' offense went, "all they've had was Freeman McNeil."

If New York goes into this game thinking they're going to do it all with Freeman McNeil, they're sadly mistaken."

With a game-time temperature of 34 degrees with an unusually bright winter sun splashing around the stadium, it was semi-tropical compared to the ill-fated playoff game against the Raiders in January 1981. The field was actually in semi-decent shape. Should be no problem for our recently acquired kicker, Mark Moseley. In our overtime win against the Steelers three weeks earlier, Matt Bahr had torn knee ligaments while making a tackle at the outset of overtime. Wondering what to do next, Ernie Accorsi, the director of football operations for the Browns, was sitting with Art Modell in the owner's booth, and saw Mark on the set of *The NFL Today*. Ernie pointed to the TV and told Art that Mark was the man for the job.

Moseley was an old pro—drafted out of Stephen F. Austin State University way back in 1970 by the Eagles. He spent a couple of years in Philadelphia and then Houston and then sat out a couple of seasons before landing in Washington. He enjoyed a stellar career—in fact, in the strike-shortened 1982 season he became the only kicker in history to win the Most Valuable Player award. On the day that I stole three passes from Terry Bradshaw in 1982, Mark set the NFL record for most consecutive field goals. In an ironic foreshadowing, Mark missed an extra point that same game.

Mark was the last of the straight-ahead kickers and used one of those 1950s-style, single-bar facemasks. He also had a thing for socks—he put five layers on his kicking foot. But at age 38, his skills were slipping, and midway through the 1986 season, the Redskins cut him loose. Mark then took the job as an analyst for CBS.

Art called the CBS studio the afternoon of the win over the goddamn Steelers. When Mark was handed a note as he came off the studio set to call the Browns, he thought it was a joke. Jimmy "The Greek" Snyder said they got crank calls like that all the time. But when Mark got home, there was another call waiting for him from Art Modell. The next day, Mark beat out three other kickers and was back on the job he loved to do.

We were zeroing in on the playoffs, and the Browns wanted someone who didn't necessarily have a 60-yard leg but could make the pressure kicks. In his 13-year career, Mark had 17 game-winning field goals and led the NFL in scoring four times.

Mark was staying in a hotel room during Thanksgiving week, when he got a call from legendary Browns kicker Don Cockroft, whom Mark had admired over the years. Don invited Mark over for Thanksgiving dinner. The turkey and stuffing did the job, when Mark got the opportunity to nail one of those pressure kicks that Sunday in his first game as a Brown. With just 18 seconds left in overtime, Mark calmly booted a 29-yarder to beat the Oilers, 13-10. Frank and I each had two picks that game. I picked off Warren Moon in the end zone to stop one drive and then got another one to set up a field goal just before halftime.

*   *   *

This day was certainly going to be a memorable for Mark—for reasons he's likely to forget and reasons he'll tell his grandchildren. It started off poorly for him on our first possession when his 46-yard attempt fell short. In the NFL, 46-yard field goals aren't supposed to fall short.

After a couple of punts, the Jets resorted to a little junior high sandlot action. Ryan tossed to McNeil, who looked like he was going to sweep around the right side, but instead he lateraled back to Ryan, who then flung it toward Wesley Walker. Walker grabbed it just as Ray Ellis hit him, but he hung on for a 42-yard score.

Then we screwed up the kickoff return, and our offense was stuck back at our own 2. But being the unflappable soldier he was, Bernie engineered a nice drive, hitting Ozzie on a couple big plays that set up a wobbly-but-great 37-yard scoring pass to Herman Fontenot.

When the Jets got the ball back, I made good plays on consecutive downs. The first on the 6-4 Al Toon, who tried to beat me down the left sideline, but I closed in when the ball was thrown and knocked it away. Then I followed Walker in motion from my right to left. Ryan tried to hit him with a square-out, but I stripped the ball away from Walker before he could get a good grip on it. We proceeded to trade field goals and went to the locker room tied, 10-10.

Another Jets field goal five minutes into the third quarter put them up, 13-10. Our offense then struggled, punting from Jets territory twice, and Mark missed to the left on a 44-yard attempt.

With the fourth quarter now upon us, we had to come up with a big drive and come away with points. But Bernie again stepped through the fire, hitting Ozzie for 33 yards, followed by a reverse to Brennan, who then threw to Webster Slaughter, then an interference call gave us the ball and a first down on the 10. Certainly within easy field-goal distance. But we wanted the TD, and we drove it all the way to the 2, where we faced a third-and-goal. Bernie backpedaled to pass. He had thrown 133 previous passes without an interception, and upon seeing nothing open, he tried to zip it out of bounds. But Bernie forgot to read the banner that read "No Red Right 88" flapping in the stadium breeze on the facing of the upper deck. He got hit as he threw. The ball fluttered through the January air, and the Jets had three defenders waiting in the corner covering Reggie and Webster. The ball landed in the hands of Jets cornerback Russell Carter.

It was one day short of six years since Red Right 88. It looked like history had just repeated itself. We knew we had to shut the Jets down and get the ball back. We bent but didn't break, and we got the ball back on our 17 with 4½ minutes to go. Bernie tried to hit Fontenot in the right flat on the first play, but cornerback Jerry Holmes picked it off and returned it to the 25. He then jogged in front of the Dawg Pound, showing off his prize, taunting the infuriated Dawg Pounders.

Then came the play that looked to be the backbreaker. McNeil took a handoff, cut through the right side, and sprinted down the sideline. I raced across the field and gave him a shove to knock him out of bounds near the goal line, but he managed to stay in and skipped in for the score. I stood there in the stunned gray silence, snapped off my helmet and slammed it to the ground. We were done, or so I thought. As did most of the other 80,000 now-frigid fans. With the extra point, we now had to score as many points in the next four minutes as we had all game, just to get into overtime. The sun was setting on the horizon and on our once-great season.

But with Bernie and these guys, you think of that 1981 Journey song "Don't Stop Believing." Center Mike Baab, who was fighting a knee strain, fired up the offense, grabbing everyone by the facemask and demanding to know who was going to be a hero. By the time Bernie trotted out to call the first play, everyone was psyched. Bernie hit Reggie Langhorne for an 8-yard pickup, but Mike was nabbed for holding, putting us in a first-and-20 situation on our 21. But later on second down, the long-haired madman Mark Gastineau (who had set an NFL record with 24 sacks in 1984), nailed Bernie after he threw, giving us another set of downs, 15 yards downfield. On a critical third down, Bernie flipped the ball to Reggie, who headed for the first-down sideline marker. The Jets managed to keep him inbounds, but a generous spot from the official gave us another first down. Bernie then hit Reggie for 13, then Brian Brennan for 23 more, then hit Brian again at the 3. After a timeout, Bernie hit Curtis Dickey out of the backfield, who made it to the 1. The two-minute warning gave our offensive coordinator, Lindy Infante, and the Jets' defensive coordinator—and future Browns head coach—Bud Carson, a moment to figure their next chess moves. Kevin Mack took the handoff and easily stepped in for a touchdown. After Mark tacked on the extra point, we were now within 3 with 1:57 left.

Since we had only two timeouts left, we had to try an onside kick. But Marion Barber cleanly fielded it on our 45. One more first down and we were done. On their first play, Carl Hairston and Bob Golic nailed McNeil in the backfield. He lost the ball, and we recovered, but the refs missed it. Still, it was a 3-yard loss. We burned our second timeout. Tony Paige came in for McNeil and got the 3 yards back, setting up a third-and-10. We called our last timeout. To this point, the Jets had converted only 2-of-14 third-down tries. This time, Sam Clancy pulled O'Brien down in the backfield on an aborted quarterback draw. We had held them. But the succeeding punt was downed on our 7, and it looked like Bernie and the boys were going to be in a huge hole. But a holding call on Barber meant the Jets had to kick it again. The Cube fielded the kick and brought it out to the 32. Fifty-three seconds were left.

Bernie threw deep over the middle for Brian, he missed it, but Carl Howard didn't miss him. Interference. We were now on the Jets' 42. Then with 47 seconds to go came a great play which I and a few others nearly fucked away. Bernie flung the ball for Webster down the left sideline. Webster had a few steps on Russell Carter, but the ball was a hair underthrown. Carter made a nice recovery and almost caught up to Webster, but Webster caught the ball just before Carter could close the gap. First-and-goal on the 5!

I was so fired up that I charged onto the field to celebrate, along with a few other teammates. What we forgot, in the midst of the excitement of the moment and booming decibels, was the fact that the clock was still running. Webster was trying to untangle himself from a defender who wouldn't let him go. Thirty-five seconds. I danced around the end zone, jumping around like a Mexican jumping bean. "That's what I'm talkin' about!" I hollered, while still bouncing around like an over-sugared 5-year-old. Twenty-five seconds. We had no timeouts. Bernie came racing down the field, gangly arms flapping, fingers pointing, yelling at everyone to line up. Webster, who had just freed himself, tried to give him a celebratory hug, but Bernie pushed him away. Twenty seconds. That's when we realized we'd better get off the damn field and fucking fast. I gathered my wits and trotted back to the sideline.

"They're going to celebrate themselves right of a football game," Criqui incredulously observed from the NBC booth. Seventeen seconds left.

Everyone was expecting Bernie to just throw the ball out of bounds to stop the clock. But Bernie had another idea. Once he aligned everyone in place, he gave a left-handed signal to Brian in the left slot, who passed on a left-handed signal to Webster split out left. Bernie dropped back and lobbed it for Webster in the left corner. But this time Carter was waiting. He leapt in the air and had the ball in his hands, only to lose it when he hit the ground. A monumental disappointment had been averted.

With 11 seconds left, Marty had seen enough. An eyewitness as Browns defensive coordinator to the original Red Right 88, he already had seen one Red Right 88 reincarnation today and saw his team come within a fingernail of a second. He didn't want to try for one more play. No more fucking around. The crowd booed as the field-goal team jogged in. Mark kicked the 22-yard field goal with seven seconds left to boot us into the seventh overtime game in playoff history. Certainly, this was one of the greatest comebacks in history.

Since regular-season overtime was instituted in 1974, we had won nine overtimes games, more than any team in the league. This was our first in postseason play.

The Jets won the toss and of course took the ball. Many in football think the team that gets the ball first in overtime usually wins. Statistics have shown that is only slightly true. The rules have changed now for the playoffs and for the regular season as well— no longer can a team "die suddenly" by a field goal on the first possession. Each team gets at least one possession, unless there is a defensive score or a touchdown.

We shut the Jets down on their first possession, sending back to the sideline with a three-and-out. Our offense then took over after the punt and marched right down the field, with Bernie hitting Reggie Langhorne with a big 35-yard pass that resembled the play to Webster that got us into overtime. Wanting to take no chances, the field-goal team came in on first down, and Mark lined up for what should have been an easy 23-yard kill shot. But the field had been thoroughly chewed up during the four-plus quarters, and when punter Jeff Gossett spotted the ball, Mark didn't get a good foothold on the loose sod, and he drew the ball wide right. No good.

Damn. We would have to go back in defensively and do it again. It would have been easy to get frustrated at that point, but Marty wasn't about to let that happen. He ordered us back on to the field before we could stand there and absorb the shock of what we just witnessed. He acted like this was just another turnover. Get our asses back out there and get the ball back.

The Jets did move on us a bit, but some big plays by Sam Clancy and Carl Hairston, the latter bagging our eighth sack of the game, snuffed out their drive. Our offense didn't do much better, and we dodged a huge bullet when Kevin Mack left the ball in the dirt deep in our own territory, but Paul Farren recovered it to save the day. We punted again, and once again, we came up big on defense. Sam nailed O'Brien for our ninth sack of the game, and we forced the Jets to punt for a record 14th time.

Our defense played as tough as ever in those overtime periods. In the Jets' last four possessions, we surrendered a total of 15 yards and one first down. They ran the ball five times for minus-4 yards, and we sacked O'Brien three times.

We got the ball back at our own 31 with just under three minutes left in the first overtime. Kevin led our offense, charging like a bull for several big pickups. The clock expired, and for only the second time in league history, there was going to be a second overtime period. Our offense confidently and coolly moved down the field, never letting the Jets get their hands on the ball. Bernie kept giving the ball to Kevin, and he kept charging through the exhausted Jets defense. Fifteen yards on a third-and-two. Then 4 more. Then 7 more. We were now perched on the Jets' 9. We and our fans realized we've seen this movie before. We were in a similar spot in the Red Right 88 game six years before. We were in this spot in the first overtime period. Those movies had very bad endings, and you could tell the buzz around the stadium was somewhat muted. Hearts were hopeful but guarded. Teeth and fists were clenched. So many fans were now conditioned to expect the worst. The field-goal team trotted on to cash this one out. The goal posts in front of the Dawg Pound resembled a mocking monument to the nightmare of Red Right 88. The Jets took a timeout, giving Mark some time to think about what just might happen—again. But this is why the Browns brought him on. Mark knew what he had to do. Physically, kicking a ball 27 yards is not that big a deal. Middle school kids can do that. But when your teammates and fans around the world are depending on you, you have to close your mind to whatever past failures lurk in your head and just do what you're supposed to do. The mental aspect can undo you in a minute. In what seemed like silence and slow motion, Mark banged the biscuit through the uprights, and we had one of the most dramatic comebacks in NFL history.

"I think we all had an opportunity to experience one of the finest games in the history of this sport," Marty said after the game. "I have never experienced or seen a comeback like that."

Ozzie Newsome played through the game with nagging injuries that suppressed his numbers (only 39 receptions) through the season, but not his heart or determination. We voted him as the winner of the Ed Block Courage Award for the year.

CHAPTER ELEVEN

Eddie and Walter

Two great men I knew over the years are two great men fate unfairly and sadly took too soon. Walter Payton, the great Bears runner, and Eddie Johnson, aka "The Assassin" aka "Bullethead." Neither of these world-class human beings would make it past their mid 40s.

I popped googly eyes when I first met Walter. He and his agent, Bud Holmes, who later became my agent, came to see me play at during my junior year of college. Both Walter and I played college football in Mississippi—he at Jackson State, graduating with a degree in communications in 1975, I at the University of Southern Mississippi, about an hour's drive away. After I signed with the Browns in 1981, Bud and I jumped on a plane to Chicago to see Walter.

We walked into Walter's house in South Barrington, Illinois, and were greeted by his trademark broad smile. His charm and charisma were surprising, considering what a punishing power runner he was. When Walter walked into a room, it was like the president of the United States had just walked in the room. Walter was the main attraction, and he wanted it that way. There was nothing wrong with that, after all, this was *the* Walter Payton. He was the man, but not in a cocky or conceited manner. He just had that personality and presence. He would greet you with a bear hug around the neck and a fiery smile that could melt diamonds.

Walter also possessed the Bill Cosby trait of making anything

funny. Cosby has that non-teachable ability to make any story funny. Sometimes I would make a wiseass remark or witty comment
in an attempt to be funny, only to get cricket chirps and yawns in
response. But Walter, just like Cosby, could use those very same
words and have the room in hysterics without even trying to be
funny. Hell, Walter could have stood in the room and recited the
fucking phone book, and it would have been funny.

"So, you just signed with the Browns?" he asked.

"Yes," I told him. "We just got it done today."

"Wow, that's great," he said, slyly looking at Bud. "You got a bonus check?"

"Sure did," I said proudly, pulling out the $150,000 check bear-
ing Art Modell's still-drying signature.

"Lemme see that bad boy," Walter said, extending his powerful
hand.

This certainly was the largest amount of money I ever saw in
one place, but I raised my chin, cracked a proud smile, and handed
over my greatest trophy to date.

"Hmmm," he muttered. He looked at me. He looked at Bud.
"One-hundred-fifty thousand dollars? Is that all?"

To me, it was just as much as $150 million. I never saw a check
with so many zeros and commas, and with my name on it, for God's
sake. And with a sparkly smile and resonant chuckle, Walter shred-
ded that check into 150,000 pieces.

I stood there, stunned, not knowing how to react. This was the
great Walter Payton, and he was fucking laughing as he was ripping
up my fucking bonus check! My agent was laughing, too. I didn't
think it was funny, but I was the rookie in the room. Walter and Bud
kept laughing, and I just looked on in horror. Motherfucker!

Walter then picked up the phone and began dialing.

"Now what the hell are you doing?" I asked incredulously.

"Just calling your boss," Walter said. In just a manner of seconds,
he had Art Modell on the line.

"Hey, Art," Walter said, bellowing with laughter between phrases. "You know that rookie you just signed? You're going to have to write him a new bonus check."

That was the way Sweetness was. Always laughing, always pranking, always smiling, always bringing cheer into the room.

Born in Columbia, Mississippi, in 1954, Walter was active in his church, Boy Scouts, and Little League baseball. He was also an excellent musician, playing drums in the John J. Jefferson High School marching band. The football coach recognized Walter's athletic ability and asked him to try out for the team. Walter agreed to do so only if he could also still play in the marching band. In his junior year, desegregation orders merged Jefferson High School with nearby Columbia High. Tensions were high, but Walter's on-field performances and off-field gentlemanlike manner helped ease the transition to an integrated South in that part of the state. This is one of the virtues of sports—success on the field can unite a community, a city, a state, even a nation. Remember what the 1980 Olympic hockey team did for a sagging American spirit?

Still in the dark ages, no Southeastern Conference school offered him a scholarship. He turned down a scholarship to the University of Kansas, the school where legendary running back Bears Gayle Sayers attended. He decided on the historically black Jackson State University, where he was given his Sweetness nickname. Achieving All-American status, Walter averaged more than 6.1 yards per carry, better than Jim Brown's collegiate average, and broke the NCAA scoring record with 65 touchdowns. He was picked by Da Bears with the fourth pick of the 1975 draft. The Falcons, Cowboys, and Colts passed on him. The Browns just missed their chance— they had the fifth pick. Could you imagine what the Kardiac Kid years would have been like had the Browns sported Walter Payton in the backfield? Had the Browns lost just one more game in their miserable 4-12 season in 1974, at the end of which they fired head coach Nick Skorich, that could have happened. On that note, the goddamn Steelers could have picked Jim Brown in the 1957 draft. They drafted one spot ahead of the Browns but picked Len Dawson.

The Browns also wanted a quarterback, but after losing a couple of coin tosses, they were stuck with the consolation prize. Could you imagine Jim Brown as a Pittsburgh Steeler? Talk about sacrilegious!

Walter and I often worked out together in the off-season. Walter rarely went into the Bears' facility to work out. He utilized his own program, which featured a series of uphill sprints. His workout habits and regimen were second to none. I was a lot younger than he was and was a bit faster, but it was hard to keep up with him. Those hills could be brutal. Many times, I wound up on the ground, puking. If anyone saw him work out, they would see why he was the great player that he was. He demanded so much out of himself and his body. He constantly pushed himself to the limit. What tremendous upper-body strength he had. He just wanted to be the best, and he was not gong to fail. He was as strong as Earl Campbell and as fast as Tony Dorsett. He could glide over a defender or knock him to the ground with a stiff arm that felt like taking a jousting shot on the chin with a telephone pole. Yet he was not one to carry on or rub it in on the field. There was no Walter Shuffle or Bears Fun Bunch. But Walter loved to have fun. Once he ran off the field ahead of all his teammates, locked the locker-room door, and took a nice long shower before letting everyone else in.

"Never Die Easy" was his motto, and the title of his posthumously released autobiography. With the will power and determination this man possessed, it was no wonder that in his legendary 13-year career he missed a grand total of one game, in his rookie year.

On the field, my teammates were aware Walter and I were good friends and business partners (we owned several night clubs around Chicago). We had an unwritten rule among us against fraternizing with the enemy. It's not that you couldn't have friends on other teams—everyone did. But as defenders, we didn't feel it was cool to hang around with wide receivers or other big offensive stars from other teams. Some of the guys accused me of not wanting to tee off on him. The guys really gave me flack, especially Frank Minnifield. But Walter and I only met on the field once, which was enough, and I played just as hard against him as I would anyone else. Da Bears beat us, 41-31, in the 1986 opener, a game which featured the first use of instant replay (and got us a touchdown—a fumble recovery in the end zone by Al Gross). Walter picked up 35 of his 113 yards on a fourth-quarter, game-clinching drive. But on the field, Walter showed me no mercy either. He would make me miss or lower his shoulder and run over me. One of my more beloved souvenirs is a picture of Walter and me standing together with our agent, Bud Holmes, after the game.

Walter retired after the 1987 season and continued his many business ventures. In addition to the night clubs we owned, Walter became a co-owner of the Dale Coyne racing team in the Indy Car World Series. He even drove in some Trans-American series races, once wrecking and suffering burns. He and several partners established the Walter Payton Roundhouse, purchasing an old railroad roundhouse in Aurora, Illinois, subsequently converting it into a restaurant, banquet facility, museum, and award-winning brewery. He also co-hosted an episode of *Saturday Night Live*.

But in early 1999, Walter was diagnosed with bile-duct cancer. He became an advocate for organ donation, although he himself was too far along in this goddamn disease to be a potential liver recipient. Walter retreated into a shell. He didn't talk to much more than his mother, wife, and brother. Having witnessed the ravaging effects of cancer on my mother and later with Eddie, I didn't want to bother him. I spoke to him last about three months before he died. It was an awkward conversation. Walter was trying to be witty, but it was now clearly a strain. I didn't see him in person, but I saw pictures and television snippets; obviously, this disease was ravaging him. We both tried to keep the conversation as light and funny as possible. We didn't discuss his illness. He knew I owned a partnership in a barge that our group was trying to sell.

"So, did you finally sell that goddamn barge?" he asked.

"Not yet. We're working on it," I said, trying to keep the conversation going.

"OK, great, call me later."

"You got it, Sweetness." Those were the last words we exchanged. On November 1, 1999, Walter died at the age of 45. A memorial service was held for him at Soldier Field in Chicago, along with a private service.

A list of Walter's accomplishments could take up half this book. But should you get the chance, get a copy of his autobiography, *Never Die Easy*, which he worked on during his final days. A hill in Arlington Heights, Illinois, has been renamed "Payton's Hill," featuring two plaques identifying it as the hill which Walter (and I) burned those uphill sprints.

*   *   *

Eddie Johnson was born in the southern Georgia town of Albany on February 3, 1959, one of eight children. He went on to star in football as a 134-pound linebacker at Dougherty High School in Albany, where he earned all-city and all-state honors, resulting in his induction in the Albany Hall of Fame in 2000. Turning down offers from Florida State and Oklahoma, Eddie attended the University of Louisville, teaming up with future fellow dawg Frank Minnifield and becoming a four-year starter. He won MVP honors and was named to the All-Metro Conference and All-South Independent teams. In one game, Eddie racked up an incomprehensible 35 tackles. Shit, 35 tackles isn't bad for a whole season, but Eddie got that in one game. He nailed over 100 tackles in each of his last three seasons. Eddie was drafted in the seventh round of the same 1981 draft that brought me to the Browns. Since we were both southerners and rookies, we had an immediate kinship.

When Eddie first came into the league, he had a bit of a chip on his shoulder, thinking he should have been drafted higher than the 187th pick. He wasn't very big, but he had 4.5 speed, very fast for a linebacker. In fact, some scouts were considering him at safety. Just for comparison, Walter Payton's 40-yard time was 4.6.

Eddie was also a tough, tough tackler, who sought out contact and loved to blow through blockers before taking down the runner. He had a ton of big hits, not only at linebacker but on special teams. In the 1986 game against the Oilers at the old stadium, Frank picked off a pass (one of two picks he nabbed in overtime), and Eddie absolutely laid out Ernest Givins. Just leveled him flat on his back. I'm surprised Ernest actually got up from that huge hit. Eddie zeroed in on those running backs and never took the direct angle to avoid contact. He wanted so much to jam that headgear through the runner. This put him and linebacker coach Dave Adolph at odds, and often they would verbally brawl. The coaches wanted it done by the book, but Eddie wanted to just knock everyone down. But Dave and Eddie loved and battled each other like a married couple.

Frank Minnifield and I often clashed with Dave as well. We would yell for more blitzes, but Dave would usually just ignore us. In the heat of battle, we often say things we really don't mean, and Dave and I yelled plenty of things at each other we really didn't mean. Very ungentlemanly exchanges, to put it mildly. A few times, I almost told him to go fuck off, but I had too much respect for the man.

One problem Eddie had was keeping up his weight. He was 6-1 and weighed about 220, and the Browns didn't want him any lighter considering the fact he would be fighting off 300-plus-pound, fire-breathing, blood-spitting madmen. One day we were lining up for weigh-ins, and I noticed an unusually large bulge in Eddie's pants. Not that I check out bulges in men's pants, but I couldn't help but notice that Eddie seemed to be a bit unusually gifted that day.

"What the hell, Bullethead?" I asked, pointing to the spot. The fans called him the Assassin, but his teammates called him Bullethead.

He then reached into his pants, flashed a 5-pound weight, and discretely dropped it back into place. I said nothing more, and no one else knew what I had witnessed. Dick Schafrath had pulled a similar stunt several years before. Dick weighed about 220 pounds, and Paul Brown wanted him to be at least 240. So Dick had a construction company in Wooster, which he once worked, put together a 25-pound jock strap held up by suspenders under his T-shirt. But Dick got busted; Eddie got away with it.

Eddie was quite a character, always joking around. He was constantly told that he was too small to play inside linebacker. But Eddie's heart made him a giant hitter.

"I'm an aggressive player," Eddie told *The Plain Dealer*. "I try not to tackle with my shoulders. I like to punish people with my head because I have more force behind it.

"The way I show leadership is by playing exciting football, making devastating hits, and hustling all the time. I want to punish the ball carrier. I want him to know who I am. You get respect that way. Every football player wants respect. This is the way I can get it."

Marty described Eddie as playing "like a man possessed." It seemed that every preseason there was speculation Eddie was going to be challenged for his starting spot, but every year, Eddie came through. Just before the 1986 season, the Browns released Tom Cousineau, the last player to be cut to reach the 45-man roster. It was a clear signal the Browns certainly had more faith in Eddie than in Tom, but it also could have been that the Browns preferred Eddie's $175,000 salary to Tom's $500,000.

I recall the 1987 training camp where Eddie was once again being challenged for the starting inside linebacker position. Anthony Griggs and Mike Johnson, along with Eddie, were battling for the two inside linebacker spots. One morning practice, Eddie lined up for our "nutcracker" drill against rookie draftee Gregg Rakoczy. The nutcracker drill is rather simple. One offensive player, one defensive player, one ball carrier. The ball carrier runs between two pads, while the defender takes on the offensive player, shedding him to get to the ball carrier. Greg tipped the scales as 285 pounds. Clearly, the physics didn't favor Eddie, but that wasn't about to intimidate Bullethead. On the whistle, Eddie charged ahead at Gregg and plowed into his midsection with a loud crack, standing the offensive lineman straight up, dead in his tracks. We barked and woofed in approval.

Later that year, Eddie saw Bernie Kosar's frustration with the play-not-to-lose offensive scheme. The week of our playoff game against the Colts, Eddie, the captain of the defense, took Bernie aside and told him to just go ahead and call his own plays or let Gary Danielson signal them in. That may seem rather insubordinate, but Eddie was doing what would give us the best chance of winning.

In his 10 years with the Browns, Eddie played in 148 of 160 games, including all 16 as a rookie. He became a starter in October 1983 when Dick Ambrose (now a judge in Cuyahoga County) broke an ankle. Eddie strung together a streak of 101 consecutive games (the franchise record is held by Doug Dieken with 203). Clay Matthews played the most number of games for the Browns—232— from 1978 to '93.

Eddie's career wound down not so much because of his playing ability, but due to pressure from the front office to work in 1987 first-round pick Mike Junkin from Duke. The Browns gave up a lot to maneuver themselves into position to take Junkin with the fifth overall pick, trading four-time Pro Bowler Chip Banks, along with their first- and second-round draft choices of 1987, to the Chargers for their first-round pick. Meanwhile, the Browns passed on future Pro Bowl linebackers Hardy Nickerson and Greg Lloyd (both snatched by the Steelers) and Shane Conlan (drafted by the Bills). Altogether, the Browns passed on two dozen future Pro Bowlers and one Hall of Famer (Rod Woodson, again drafted by those goddamn Steelers) to take Junkin, whose career unfortunately turned out to be analogous to his surname. After two unremarkable years with the Browns and one abbreviated season with Kansas City, he was out of football. Junkin was called "a mad dog in a meat market," but he turned out to be more of a puppy found at a flea market.

The Browns unloaded Mike on draft day the following year to the Chiefs, where ironically he would follow Marty, who had resigned after the 1988 season and then took the head coaching job in Kansas City. Mike lasted five games, and his career was over. Ernie Accorsi, Browns director of football operations, had to admit that "he had a bad experience here, and it was a bad experience for us."

A 1989 story in *The Plain Dealer* said the Browns drafted the Mad Dog "with the full knowledge he had tested positive for steroids." Hmm, he came out of high school as a 189-pound tight end but wound up a 240-pound linebacker. Nothing suspicious there, I'm sure. And the fact that he held out for over two weeks at the beginning of training camp until he became the top-paid linebacker certainly did nothing to ingratiate himself with the team, coaches and fans. Mike did make one nice play, sort of, in an exhibition game against the Packers. He picked off a pass and ran it in for the winning score, but, indicative of his truncated career, the only reason he made the play is because he blew the coverage on the tight end and was out of position.

I don't know why the Browns developed some fetish for blowing first-round draft picks on linebackers who go bust. The Browns then drafted Clifford Charlton out of the University of Florida the next year. He was also done in two years. Then in 1995, like a dog to its vomit, the Browns took Craig Powell out of Ohio State with their first-round pick. Soon after, Powell tore up his knee and was out of the league after three years. Altogether, those three first-round draft choices amassed a grand total of zero interceptions, zero fumble recoveries, zero forced fumbles and one sack in their combined careers of 6½ years. The Browns passed on 61 future Pro Bowlers and two future Hall of Famers to get these guys. When the Plan B list of protected and unprotected free agents came out in February 1989, Eddie was left unprotected. Mike was not.

Earnest Byner told a story of one of his first meetings with Eddie, detailed in *Plain Dealer* reporter Tony Grossi's book, *Tales from the Browns Sidelines*. "Gary Danielson tossed the ball to me and I started to the outside and decided to downhill full speed. WHAP!

That's what you heard. I didn't move and the person in front of me didn't move. It was Eddie. I remember looking into his eyes. Those glazing, big, white, intense, beautiful eyes."

It seemed that every year someone was challenging Eddie for his starting position. After the Junkin debacle, the Browns signed 10-year pro Barry Krauss, who played for the Indianapolis-Baltimore Colts. The speculation was he was going to replace Eddie, but Krauss didn't make it through training camp and was shipped off to the Dolphins. The Colts then tried to sign away Eddie, but he stayed with the Browns for his final two seasons, even though he would have made more money in Indy.

Eddie retired after the abysmal 3-13 season the Browns slogged through in 1990, making his career one year longer than mine. I got to know him and his beautiful family—his wife, Terri, whom Eddie married 20 days before he died, and his three kids, Rahshan, Elise, and Elexis. Just beautiful people, all of them. I also got to know his mother fairly well; he rarely spoke of his father. Eddie also talked a lot about his brother, whom he loved dearly, but who was in prison. After football, Eddie took up golf and became very good at it—toting a single-digit handicap. He practiced constantly. He also was a sharp pool player, using his own custom cue stick, and winning a few tournaments. I often shot pool with him, but compared to him, I wasn't worth a tinker's damn. He also loved bass fishing.

He was a most caring and dedicated soul to charitable causes, especially when kids were involved. He served as the honorary chairman of a Diabetes Association swimathon and raised money for the March of Dimes and the Big Brothers and Sisters program.

Eddie and I hung out with Judson Flint, Cleo Miller, and Larry Friday. But Eddie for some reason claimed to be the originator of the Dawg Pound. He was there at the beginning, yes, and the Pound loved him, but there's no mistaking that the Pound thing was clearly Frank's and my baby. Somehow, Cleo and Judson went along with Eddie on this. Cleo would always say to Eddie, "Why don't you tell Hanford how the Dawgs really got started?"

One theory is that Eddie, instead of telling you that you did a good job, would just call you a dawg. After a while, he'd just bark at you. He was also from Georgia and grew up rooting for the Georgia Bulldogs. We'd go to soul food restaurants and have a drink together. I attended Harvest Missionary Baptist Church on East 93rd Street with Eddie, who was the associate pastor, and his family. Eddie entered the ministry in 1993. He also got involved in the building business and also considered getting back into football in some front office capacity. He was a coaching intern with the Browns' training camp and also performed some duties in the personnel department.

Eddie had a great compassion for his brother Charles, who was in state prison in Georgia by the time Eddie was 9. This compassion got Eddie into some trouble after he retired from football. Charles turned out to be a career criminal, sentenced to two life terms without parole, with a criminal record dating back to 1968. On July 31, 1995, while in Crisp County Jail in Cordele, Georgia, Charles and three other inmates used smuggled hacksaws to cut through bars and vents and escape through the prison duct works. Charles then came to Cleveland, specifically to Eddie's home in Brook Park, and Eddie tried to help him. Clearly, his compassion for his brother, while understandable, was misplaced. But Eddie was driven by the love and compassion he had for him. I'm sure Eddie allowed him in his house not to accommodate Charles' criminal enterprises or to callously disregard the law, but because he truly believed, to a fault, that he could find a way to fix his big brother's troubles. That's the way Eddie thought and lived.

The authorities caught Charles just outside Eddie's house and charged Eddie with harboring a fugitive. That could have put him away for five years, but he wound up getting a year's probation.

One day in November 2000, I got a phone call. One of those damn phone calls you hope you never have to take. "There's something you need to hear from me before you hear it from anyone else," he said slowly. "I've got cancer."

"Oh, fuck, Bullethead," I said. "Tell me you're shittin' me."

"No, Dawg," he said. "I've got it in the colon. I've known about for about a month, and I've been trying to figure out how to handle it."

"So what's your game plan?" I asked, hand to my forehead.

"I'm going to fight this thing with all I've got," he said most determinedly. I would expect nothing less from this ferocious gentleman.

"How far along is it?" I asked.

"They're still trying to determine that right now, but I'll let you know. I'm in the finest hands with some of the finest doctors at Cleveland Clinic." That he was, but a few weeks later, he told me that the cancer was pretty far along. When I saw him, I could see that his once steel-twined body was being eaten up from within. Eddie, whose father died of colon cancer in 1962 at age 62, underwent surgery and actually was better for a bit over a year. But the cancer came roaring back, reoccurring in his pelvis and lungs. He kept fighting with all the strength and determination he could muster.

On a cold and snowy January 21, 2003, I stood in Eddie's Cleveland Clinic hospital room, along with Reggie Langhorne, Ricky Feacher, Herman Fontenot, Felix Wright, and, Eddie's beautiful wife and children. He raised his head up and weakly pulled off his oxygen mask with his once-powerful but now frail-and-trembling hand.

"I just can't do it anymore," he said with a hoarse whisper. He laid his head back, closed his eyes, and an hour later quietly crossed the bridge from this world to the next. It was an incredibly sad moment, and his kids, all teenagers, took it really hard. Eddie was all of 43 years old. Shit, cancer just sucks.

At the 2½-hour funeral, held at Church on the Rise in Westlake before some 750 mourners, Bernie Kosar, one of the 15 who eulogized Eddie, called him "The Captain" and told the story about Eddie being "screwed over" by the Browns with the Mike Junkin affair.

Mary Vukich, a 9-year-old survivor of multiple brain tumors who became an inspiration for Eddie, played her violin. Eleven-year-old Cory Fritz had organized a bowling benefit for Eddie, returning the favor from when Eddie raised money for Cory's needed heart transplant. Cory broke down while being interviewed. Johnny Davis graced the service with his fluid keyboard work, and Cleo Miller melodiously sang "The Lord's Prayer."

In his memory, the Eddie Johnson Foundation became the Eddie Johnson Memorial Foundation. It carries on one of Eddie's passions—helping the less fortunate. The foundation has funded important work such as school bags for children, medical bills for heart transplant victims, customizing houses for the handicapped, food and housing for families in transition and numerous other crises-intervening causes. Reggie Langhorne now heads up the foundation.

The stories of Walter Payton and Eddie Johnson parallel the standard plot of a Hemingway novel—brave men doing great things, but not surviving the outcome. This begs the age-old question: Why do such bad things happen to such good people? I'm not going to begin to answer that question. It's something we will ponder and debate until the end of time. Perhaps in the end, whenever or whatever that will be, we will come to an understanding then.

CHAPTER TWELVE

The Drive

The week leading up to the game was just crazy. For the first time since the 1969 season, the era of Bill Nelsen and Leroy Kelly, the Browns were one victory away from the Super Bowl. Everyone was still hung over from the incredible double-overtime victory over the Jets just a week before, but the town was buzzing, getting ready for the AFC Championship Game on January 11, 1987.

Banners hung from everywhere, including the control tower at the airport. Browns helmets were found on statues downtown. Bridal shops offered specials on orange-and-brown gowns. Songs and ditties about the Browns filled the airwaves. At the end of their performance, members of the Cleveland Orchestra began barking. A district judge used the Browns as an example of what was great about America while swearing in a group of new citizen immigrants. Even Johnny Carson chimed in during one of his *Tonight Show* monologues. "The Cleveland Browns in a championship?" he asked. "The last time the Browns were in the playoffs, Cleveland wasn't a city. It was a president."

WMMS DJ Ed "Flash" Ferenc let his listeners know that the Broncos had checked into the Stouffer Hotel on Public Square in downtown Cleveland—and encouraged fans to drive around that hotel all night long and blast their horns. Some even wiggled their way through security and ran through the hotel hallways, screaming, yelling, and barking.

Hundreds of frosty fans camped outside of the Cleveland

Browns ticket office in Tower B of Cleveland Stadium. Tickets went on sale Monday morning at 8:30 a.m. and were gone in a couple hours. Scalpers were getting anywhere from $85 to $150 a clip.

The Broncos had never won a playoff game on the road, and everyone was confident this was finally, finally the year that Cleveland would shed its image of "the mistake by the lake." The grounds crew coated the goal posts with furniture polish to make it difficult for onrushing fans to tear them down after the certain Browns grand victory.

The day before the game, Broncos kicker Rich Karlis wanted to get on the field to practice a few kicks, but found the field covered with the tarp. He was told the tarps had to stay on to protect the grass. But as the Broncos took the field the next day, Karlis realized that "they were only keeping the green dirt protected because there was no grass."

But we knew the Broncos were going to be tough. They had a solid defense, led by Rulon Jones, the AFC Defensive Player of the Year, and linebacker Karl Mecklenburg. Their offense began and ended with John Elway, although there were rumblings in the media that Elway was a bit overrated. That sentiment was echoed by *The Plain Dealer's* Bob Dolgan, who wrote, "In truth, Elway is overrated. He has not yet arrived as a first-class operator. The voters must have been dreaming when they put him into the Pro Bowl as Dan Marino's substitute."

The numbers did make a case that Elway had underperformed. After coming out of Stanford in 1983 (he led Stanford to a lead against California that was wiped out by the infamous lateral-through-the-marching-band, game-ending play), Elway was drafted by the Baltimore Colts. But he wanted nothing to do with their coach, Frank Kush, who had a history of clashing with players and administrators throughout his collegiate and professional coaching career. Kush was sued by a former Arizona Sun Devil for harassment and punching him in the mouth after a bad punt. He also ran into trouble while coaching the Hamilton Tiger Cats of the

Canadian Football League by trying to ban the taping of ankles. Elway tersely demanded he either had to be traded or he would continue his baseball career in the New York Yankees organization. The Colts really had no choice, so they traded Elway to Denver for tackle Chris Hinton and quarterback Mark Herrmann.

Elway quickly became the starter in Denver as a rookie but just completed 47.5 percent of his passes for an abysmal passer rating of 54.9. He did progress over the next three years, but his passer rating never exceeded 80. In contrast, Bernie had a 69.3 rating his first year, 83.8 his second, and would rack up a 95.4 rating his third year.

The consensus was that Bernie was better than Elway. Dolgan wrote, "Kosar reminds you of a lethal poker player, with his tight lips and flat eyes," and Elway "looks like the trusting boy next door going out for a malted milk." His feet were the one advantage Elway had, although he had a bit of a sore ankle coming into the game. He was quick and fluid, and turned many would-be-loss plays into first downs with his cat-like reflexes and quarter-horse speed. Bernie looked a bit like a whooping crane when he ran, but his smarts, coolness under pressure, laser-point accuracy, and ability to beat the blitz made him the top-shelf quarterback he was.

The Broncos started the season 8-1 but lost four of their last seven games. Their 11-5 record was good enough to win the AFC West title, aided by the late-season woes of the Los Angeles Raiders.

The Plain Dealer also reported 22 of 29 sportswriters around the country predicted we would win. Every football writer at *The Plain Dealer* concurred. The oddsmakers had us a three-point favorite. Bengals coach Sam Wyche predicted victory for us.

The only things gray and dingy that day were the sky and stadium structure. The mighty Ohio State Marching Band marched on the field before the game, forming a "Script Browns" for the occasion. The table was set. The Dawg Pound was in full battle gear, and several Broncos—including owner Pat Bowlen, nestled in his full-length man fur coat, who strayed too close during the pregame warm-ups—got pelted with biscuits.

"Hey, can they get away with this?" Broncos receiver Steve Watson kept asking.

Just before the kickoff, Marty gave us his famous "There's a gleam, men," speech.

We wasted no time scoring first. On our second possession, Bernie, with snowflakes blowing in off the lake, marched us 86 yards. That drive almost ended in a turnover, but Tucker recovered Kevin Mack's fumble at the Denver 6. On the next play, Bernie swung a pass to Herman Fontenot in the right flat, and he juked Tony Lilly on the frosty green dirt and danced in the end zone. We had the lead and the momentum. But bad things come in threes—and we turned the ball over on our next three possessions. The Broncos finally converted one into points—with us missing a man, Gerald Willhite sailed into the end zone on a fourth-and-goal from the 1 after Elway had scrambled for 34. But we came back with a field goal late in the first half and went into the locker room tied, 10-10.

Midway through the third quarter, Mark Harper picked off Elway at the sideline on our 31, and instant replay upheld the call. But offensively, we stalled again and punted away.

This time the Broncos marched down the field, and Karlis punched in a 26-yard field goal to give Denver a three-point lead, which they took into the fourth quarter. But Bernie led another fine drive down to the Broncos' 8, and Mark Moseley straight-toed another three-pointer to tie the game.

Defensively, we stuffed them two more series, both of them three-and-outs, and after a fine punt return by Gerald "Ice Cube" McNeil, we were set up at our own 48 with 6:40 to go. After an incomplete pass and a 4-yard pickup by Herman, Bernie came up to the line of scrimmage on third-and-6. The call was "two flip wide, Y option, X smash." He spotted a blitz. This meant that the wily Brian Brennan would be one-on-one with Dennis Smith, who had missed the previous week's playoff victory over New England with a bad knee. Bernie let it fly toward the left sideline. It was underthrown, but Brian adjusted his pattern perfectly and came back for it, while Smith got his feet tangled up beneath him. Brian caught the ball, juked to the inside, juked to the outside and breezed past Smith's strewn carcass into the end zone.

That was it. Eighty-thousand fans, and millions more on TV, just knew that we were headed to the Super Bowl. So did the NBC television crew. They began to set up their equipment at the entrance to our locker room where soon we would be hoisting the Lamar Hunt Trophy. Bernie and Brian had just pulled off the greatest play in the history of great plays. For sure, the statue of General Moses Cleaveland (that's how he spelled his name) on Public Square was now dancing a jig. One hundred-ninety years of scorn, disappointment, default, burning rivers, *Laugh-In* jokes, and Johnny Carson barbs were about to end.

The ensuing kickoff only confirmed it. Moseley kicked the ball—the last and greatest kick of his career. It wasn't a clean kick—it was a knuckler—but it knuckled the right way. Gene Lang, backup running back for the Broncos, watched the ball hit on the 23 and bounce toward the end zone. Lang misplayed it, the ball scooted by and he finally cradled the free ball at the 2, only to be snowed over by an avalanche of white jerseys.

"That's it. Three-and-out. Three-and-out!" I yelled as I snapped on my chin strap and ran on the field. In the defensive huddle, that's what we kept telling each other. The Broncos needed a touchdown, and they had just over five minutes to go 98½ yards. We had them jailed back almost as far as possible. Just close out this one series, and we're in the Super Bowl.

We had done a fairly good job of keeping Elway in check. He had completed only 14 of 26 passes for 116 yards and had gotten just 36 yards on the ground to this point. They scored 10 of their 13 points on short fields following a turnover. They had picked up a measly 21 yards on their past two possessions. All the math, all the momentum, all the karma had us booking plane tickets for Pasadena, California, for the Super Bowl. Now we knew how the Jets felt the week before after McNeil's touchdown. And soon—I know I'm not revealing an ending we already are too painfully aware of—we would feel like the Jets after Mark's game-winner.

Broncos guard Keith Bishop later told his teammates in the huddle, "We've got 'em right where we want them."

First of all, let me make this clear: Yes, we would eventually use the so-called prevent defense, and over the years I've heard over and over the very tired cliché that all the prevent defense prevents is a win. But in this situation and circumstance, it was absolutely the right call. If you don't go to the prevent, or "nickel" coverage when the offense is very likely to pass, then you run the risk of a mismatch—a linebacker could be left to cover a speedy back coming out of the backfield or even a wide receiver. That, of course, would be an instant disaster. The prevent defense, or Cover 7 as we called it, works if executed properly. Our trouble with it is that we—especially I—made some key mistakes at critical times.

First-and-10 from the Denver 2.

This was a situation where if we were aggressive, we could knock them back for a safety, effectively ending the game; however, if we were overly aggressive, they could rip off a big play and get out of trouble. We stayed in our usual 3-4 defense, which had been effective all day. Elway faked a handoff to Gerald Willhite and rolled to the left through the end zone and encountered no pressure. He fired the ball to Sammy Winder in front of me. I took him down inbounds, keeping the clock running. Pickup of 5 yards, no real big deal.

Second-and-5 from the Denver 7.

Winder took a sweep to the left side and picked up 3 yards. The Broncos took their first timeout.

Third-and-2 from the Denver 10.

Here was our first chance to snuff out these suckers. Winder took the ball for 2 yards, and it was going to depend on the spot. They brought out the chains—first down by an inch. Dammit.

First-and-10 from the Denver 12.

Winder for 3 yards. Clock keeps running. We're still in pretty good shape.

Second-and-7 from the Denver 15.

We wanted to get some pressure on Elway, so we stacked six on the line. We had great coverage, and the pocket collapsed. Elway eluded the rush and found a seam on the left side, picking up 11 yards.

First-and-10 from the Denver 26.

The Broncos called a "Fire Pass 94." Elway faked a handoff and fired a throw to Steve Sewell, who jumped high to flag down the high pass. He grabbed it, and Chris Rockins cut his legs out, flipping the former first-round pick on his back. He held on to the ball for a 22-yard gain. The Broncos were now at midfield, and we, along with the nearly 80,000 chilled fanatics, began to get a bit nervous.

First-and-10 from the Denver 48.

We blitzed Clay Matthews, who chased Elway in the pocket. But he got pushed aside and missed Elway, who then fired a 12-yarder toward Steve Watson. Frank Minnifield had the hook route well-covered, but Watson used his 6-4 height over Frank's 5-9 to wrestle the ball away. Now this was getting serious. I wasn't chipping and yakking at the receivers at this point. I needed to concentrate on what I had to do. Yakking at Watson didn't do much good, as he ignored it just as much as John Stallworth of the goddamn Steelers had ignored it.

First-and-10 from the Cleveland 40.

This time, we blitzed Chip Banks, and Elway got hit by Bob Golic as he released the ball for Vance Johnson down the right sideline. Incomplete.

Second-and-10 from the Cleveland 40.

Elway didn't get away this time. Matthews blitzed again, and backup nose tackle Dave Puzzuoli wrapped him up for an 8-yard sack, his seventh of the season. We felt the momentum shift back to us. They now faced a third-and-long. Denver took its second time-out.

Third-and-18 from the Cleveland 48.

Shit, this was the backbreaker. We had five guys in man-to-man coverage and two safeties deep. Elway was in the shotgun, and Watson, who was lined up in the backfield, came in motion to the right. As he passed between Elway and the center, the center snapped the ball, mistiming the motion and the silent cadence. The ball skipped off Watson's left ass cheek. Watson looked back to see where the ball was heading, but like a hockey goalie or a baseball catcher, Elway deftly made the save before the ball hit the ground. Mark Jackson came at me. I tried to jam him to the outside, but did so too aggressively. Jackson slipped to my inside. We were in a Cover 6, and I never had let anyone get inside me on a Cover 6. I knew Elway would spot him, and he did. I recovered enough to hit Jackson, and Felix Wright brought him down. But it was a damn 20-yard gain. The Broncos lucked out, I fucked up, and we were up shit creek. This is the nightmare that haunts me to this damn day. They were now on our 28, with a buck-twenty-four left. The television crew started to break down the equipment they had set up outside our locker room.

First-and-10 from the Cleveland 28.

Elway throws another incompletion, trying to find Watson down the right sideline.

Second-and-10 from the Cleveland 28.

Another blitz, another Elway dance. He soft-shoed his way out of trouble and hit Sewell for 14 yards on a screen pass to the left side.

First-and-10 from the Cleveland 14.

Watson tried to catch one over Minnifield in the corner of the end zone, but Frank had it well covered. Watson caught the ball but out of bounds.

Second-and-10 from the Cleveland 14.

Watson started off in motion again, we blitzed, and again, Elway stayed one step ahead. He slipped through the right side for a 9-yard gain. That really hurt us. Elway can hurt you in so many ways. We were looking at each other, talking to each other, desperate to make a big play. No question the Broncos had us on our heels.

Third-and-1 from the Cleveland 5.

The 15th and final, fatal play. The Dawg Pound stood behind us, yelling with everything they could muster. We were in the nickel, and Jackson went in motion from the slot. The Broncos called the "option 62 left rebel." Jackson, who wasn't the primary receiver, ran a "rub" pattern, then broke open to the middle on the slant, and Elway's eyes grew as big as Frisbees. He smoked the ball just over Carl Hairston's right hand but down and away so that if Jackson didn't catch it, no one would. Sliding on his knees, Jackson got the catch and the damn touchdown. We stood there, wooden-faced, shaking our heads. How the hell did these bastards just march 98 fucking yards on us? It had to have been a higher power at work. Somewhere in the cosmos, it was predestined that the Broncos were going to win that game, no matter what we did.

*   *   *

One thing a lot of people forget is that The Drive didn't win the game for the Broncos. There were still 37 seconds left, and many things, good or bad, can happen in that span. Gerald McNeil fielded the kickoff off a funny bounce and brought it back only 3 yards to our 15. Bernie then threw an innocuous pass to Herman for 4 yards, then kneeled down. We would take our chances in overtime.

We won the toss, and our offense was determined to go out there and win it quickly. But this time, it was a three-and-out as Herman got stuffed on a third-and-2, and we had to punt it away.

So after getting the life sucked out of us on The Drive, we had to go out there and find it within us to stop them this time. It was sort of a do-over. An opportunity to reverse fortune. But it also presented an opportunity for me to fuck up again.

After the punt, the Broncos had it on their own 25. Elway threaded the needle to rookie Orson Mobley, who made a great falling catch for 22 yards. But we held them to a third-and-12 situation. I lined up over Watson and tried to jam him as he broke off the line. He gave me a juke, but I turned and stayed with him. Then I saw

Elway rolling my way. In a split second, I had to decide whether to stay with Watson or let him go and take a shot at Elway. But I hesitated. I wasn't sure if Felix Wright was going to come over from his safety position quickly enough to cover Watson. But it looked like Elway had passed the line of scrimmage, so I left Watson and drew a bead on Elway while Watson worked his way behind me. But I had misjudged Elway's position. He wasn't yet past the line. Just before Elway reached the line of scrimmage, he pulled up and flung the ball to Watson. I leapt in the air but couldn't get it. Felix got over there a fraction of a second too late and delivered a big hit, but Watson hung on, and the Broncos were in business on our 22. Chip Banks tore a hamstring on that play, the last play of his career with the Browns.

Three runs later, they sent in the field-goal team. Karlis, who was from nearby Salem, Ohio, and was another one of those screwball barefoot kickers, hooked the ball, but it still slipped in just inside the upright for the 23-20 win. The Broncos were going to the Super Bowl, the one that just a few minutes ago we thought would be ours.

The stadium went as cold and quiet as the ice box it was. But as we trudged our way off the field and toward the first base dugout, the fans rose to their feet and cheered appreciatively. We tried to take solace in that, but still, the experience was devastating. We sat around the locker room in stunned silence, and I wouldn't be surprised if there weren't a few hidden tears. But there were no theatrics, there was no wailing, there were no slamming fists, there was no blaming others. We were just too tired, too stunned, too drained. The press was then let in, and nobody ducked any questions. Meanwhile, the Broncos were parading around in their locker room with their AFC champion T-shirts and hats. In our stadium. Fuck.

*   *   *

"Being mature stinks," Mike Baab told the media. "I wanted so bad to throw my helmet and let it all out."

Legendary *Plain Dealer* football writer Chuck Heaton wrote, "In many years of Browns watching, there have been tough losses as well as great victories. But I don't think there was a more difficult defeat to watch or harder story to write than that on Jan. 11, 1987."

The Broncos went on to the Super Bowl in Pasadena two weeks later, only to be trounced by the New York Giants, 39-20.

All these years later, it still smarts for all of us. If only I hadn't let Jackson get to my inside. If only that snap would have hit the meatier part of Watson's ass. Then the city would have bright murals of that Bernie-to-Brian play sandblasted and sealed onto the side of every warehouse. Instead, Elway got a full display of The Drive in the Hall of Fame, which, as of this writing, is still there. And on Public Square, the statue of Moses Cleaveland patiently waits for that magical moment to come to life.

The Drive was featured in the 2010 movie *Hot Tub Machine*, and in the movie, due to some alteration of past events, Jackson drops that fucking pass and we go on to the Super Bowl. How I wish life really did imitate art.

CHAPTER THIRTEEN

Dawg Days

Frank Minnifield and I stood on the steps of the Cuyahoga County Courthouse in downtown Cleveland. We were dressed in Superman-like costumes, capes fluttering in the summer breeze. The photographer snapped a bunch of pictures. I had "TD" on the front of my outfit, obviously for "Top Dawg." Frank had "MM" on the front of his getup, standing for "Mighty Minnie." This fashion shoot led to our poster that came out in November 1987, right in the middle of another great year.

The 1987 season was a great one overall, but it was a season of great peaks and valleys, for the Browns, the league, and me. It started off odd enough with the draft-day trade with San Diego that sent Chip Banks for a first-round draft choice to pick Mike Junkin. I loved playing behind Chip. I think Chip and Clay Matthews were the best linebacker combination in the league—equivalent to Frank and me at cornerback. Chip seemed to think Marty favored Clay, and Chip also seemed to be always asking for more money, thus he was deemed a bit of a troublemaker and therefore expendable.

The trade was conditional—either Penn State's Shane Conlan or Junkin had to be available when the Browns picked fifth. Both Conlan and Junkin were still on the board when the Browns came on the clock. Don Anile, one of our scouts, is the one who originally called Mike the "mad dog in a meat market." Marty Schottenheimer was similarly swooning over Mike, going so far as to say he was the best linebacker since Lawrence Taylor and that Mike reminded him of Jack Lambert. I kid you not. And so the pick was made.

Losing Chip was very costly to us, and putting Mike in his place meant that Mike was going to have to make the switch from inside linebacker to outside, which requires a different skill set that's even more pronounced at the NFL level. Mike and his holdout dominated the headlines during training camp. After a 16-day, 23-practice stalemate, he came to camp and in his first practice showed that he could hit, leveling running back Major Everett on a 16-tag-trap play. But too often, Mike was either confused or frustrated. In our first exhibition game, against the Giants in East Rutherford, New Jersey, Mike's very first play turned out to foreshadow the direction of his career. He ran about 40 yards across and down the field in pursuit of O.J. Anderson and delivered a big hit, but out of bounds. Personal foul, Number 54, defense.

Despite having more tackles in his senior season at Duke than Conlan and Alabama's Cornelius Bennett combined, Mike quickly flamed out, and Conlan enjoyed three All-Pro years with the Bills and Rams, as well as being named NFL Defensive Rookie of the Year.

We helped our offense by drafting offensive lineman Gregg Rakoczy out of the University of Miami in the second round and fullback Tim Manoa, another Penn State product, in the third round.

Defensively, we traded with the Cardinals to get Al "Bubba" Baker, a rather colorful personality—to say the least—to help the pass rush. With Anthony Griggs taking Chip's spot at left outside linebacker and Sam Clancy getting his first start at defensive end, we were rebuilding the left side of our defense. We engaged in an intense off-season conditioning program, unlike any I had ever seen before. We pushed each other in the off-season not just to stay in shape but to come back bigger and stronger than before. From March until May minicamp, only eight veterans stayed outside of Cleveland, two of whom were kickers. Our strength coach, Dave

"Red Man" Redding, worked us hard. Believe it or not, we were paid $50 a day to come in and lift. The money obviously wasn't the inspiration. We believed that just a few more sit-ups, a few more bench presses, and a few more squats could make the inch-and-a-half difference between getting to the Super Bowl and staying home yet again. The New York Giants had been working a similar program, and in two years, none of their regular offensive linemen had missed a game.

The fans and the city were still in euphoria from the record number of wins in the 1986 season, and by midsummer, the Browns had already sold some 50,000 season tickets. "We, in the front office, are talking Super Bowl," Art Modell told the media. "My feelings are of great, great anticipation and expectation. I feel we're a better team than before."

*   *   *

Camp was run like a minimum-security prison. There were curfews and bed checks. Frank got married on July 25 and had been with his wife only two days total during camp, which closed August 28. Then he had to get a wisdom tooth pulled.

Cody Risien, who went to the Pro Bowl the previous season, was a holdout but signed a two-year deal just before our third exhibition game in Atlanta. The same day that Cody reached his deal, the Browns waived special teams captain and player representative Curtis Weathers. Releasing our player rep just before a looming strike might have raised a few eyebrows, but no one really suspected anything devious on the part of the Browns. Curtis remained our player rep until we elected Mike Pagel as his replacement at the beginning of the regular season. The Patriots, though, traded Brian Holloway to the L.A. Raiders for a draft choice the day after Holloway spoke on behalf of the NFLPA on national television. Hmmm.

Tim was named the outstanding rookie of camp. He was awarded the Maurice Bassett Award, named after the battering-ram fullback who followed Marion Motley and preceded Jim Brown. Tim was the 80th pick of the draft and exceeded expectations. The football soothsayers at *The Plain Dealer* unanimously picked us to win the division.

While Mike and Cody's holdouts were a minor distraction, other holdouts among our division foes were rather acrimonious. Alonzo Highsmith, Houston's top pick and fourth overall, was asking a million dollars more than the Oilers were willing to pay. The goddamn Steelers wrote off cornerback Rod Woodson, the 10th overall pick. The Bengals were in a stalemate with their top pick, Jason Buck, and All-Pro tackle Anthony Munoz.

With Bernie Kosar a year more experienced, the second season for offensive coordinator Lindy Infante, Ozzie Newsome back in good health, and the prospect of Earnest Byner and Kevin Mack back together in the backfield, optimism correspondingly ran extra high.

Eddie Johnson, who had watched "The Drive" from the sideline while clutching his ribs, was ready at full strength, hitting everyone and everything in sight, as usual.

At our first exhibition game, against the St. Louis Cardinals, 78,650 fans showed up, the largest exhibition crowd in 16 years. We cruised to a 31-16 win, mostly on the second-half efforts of the second- and third-teamers.

But there was plenty of trouble brewing on the horizon. The labor agreement between the players and the league was expiring August 31, and talks were getting nowhere fast. The owners were already gearing up to establish replacement teams if there was a strike. Several players who were cut during training camp were given $1,000 bonuses to bind their contracts over in case of a strike.

*   *   *

Meanwhile, back in Alabama, my mother was having serious health issues. At age 51, she was battling cancer. She had surgery to remove a tumor on her liver. It was very difficult for me to stay up in Ohio while my mother was going through the struggles she was bravely enduring. Fortunately, my sister Debra was there, along with my dad. I kept in constant contact with them. Mentally, it was very hard to stay focused on football. Physically, I was dealing with another nagging groin pull, but I was ready to go for the season opener.

"On paper, this could be one of the best teams the Browns have fielded—on paper now—since I bought the club in 1961," Art told *The Plain Dealer*.

We opened the season with the deck stacked against us. We traveled to New Orleans to take on the much-improved Saints in the Superdome. The day before the game, the pope celebrated a mass in the Superdome, the home of a team called the Saints. So we had a tough act to follow, and the Saints were aware of our left side-issues. They attacked accordingly, running second-year running back Reuben Mayes at our left side for 104 of his 147 yards. We could only get to quarterback Bobby Hebert only once. Despite our defensive struggles, Bernie Kosar kept our offense moving, and with 12:37 to go, the score was 21-21. But Bernie got nailed for two fourth-quarter safeties, and along with a field goal, the Saints prevailed, 28-21. For the fifth straight year, we started the season 0-1, and making matter worse, all of our division rivals won their openers. And the next week, we had to take on the goddamn Steelers at home.

The Saturday night before the game, I got a phone call from my sister Debra. It was solemn.

"Momma is on life support," she softly uttered. "She has taken a bad turn. I hate to have to tell you this the night before such a big game, but you better get on the next plane and get down here if you want to see here alive one more time."

Very few things could mess up someone's mind just before a game more than that. A big part of preparation is to have your mind clear and focused, both on the emotional side and the technical side. To get a call like that just totally fucked with my head in the worst way, and just before a big game with the goddamn Steelers. I kept telling myself that I was a professional, and I could get through this. I did the best I could, but try as I might, I couldn't separate the thoughts and concern for my mother from my game preparation. Sunday morning came and there was no change in my mother's condition, so I made my way to the Stadium and tried to focus as best I could.

Marty, defensive coordinator Dave Adolph and secondary coach Bill Cowher, our fourth secondary coach in four years, watched the Bears stuff the Super Bowl champion Giants on *Monday Night Football* and came up with a hybrid of Chicago's 4-6 defense. I guess you could say the Dawg Defense went to the Bear Defense. We switched out of the 3-4 defense with an occasional fourth lineman, a third cornerback, and would bring in one of the safeties to function as a fifth linebacker. It worked beautifully. We shut down the goddamn Steelers in Week 2, holding them to 58 rushing yards, and 29 yards total offense in the second half, only 3 of them on the ground. We picked off Mark Malone and Bubby Brister a combined total of six times, with Chris Rockins and Clay Matthews each snagging two. Clay returned one for a 26-yard score as we cruised, 34-10. Frank picked off a pass and returned it to the 1 as time expired.

Everything was now beginning to align as we knew it could. But now, everything was about to fall apart, in the league and at home. There was no 11th-hour deal between the players and the league. In fact, between August 14 and September 8, the two sides had met for only 4½ hours. The strike was on.

In the locker room after our win over the goddamn Steelers, I was quiet and subdued. In our postgame prayer, Marty mentioned my mother. He told the press about the situation, fighting back tears. Reporters were asking Frank questions as he stood next to me. I just quickly got dressed and got out of there. I knew there would be some very difficult decisions my sister and Dad and I would have to make over the next few days. Decisions I knew I would dread having to make. I gave Frank a little bag and told him to hang on to it for me. While I was sympathetic to the guys and would have joined them on the picket line the following week, I left the Stadium and drove straight to the airport, hopping on a plane for Mobile, Alabama.

*   *   *

We went on strike mostly out of loyalty to the other guys in the league and for the betterment of the guys who would be playing in the future. In all honesty, we weren't gung-ho about going out on strike, unlike in 1982. The main reason, as far as the players' association was concerned, was free agency. Once a player's contract expired, he was free to negotiate with any other team, but the original club had the right to match that offer. But that artificially drove the price way up for a new team to sign someone, so the market pretty much wasn't there. In fact, over the past 10 years, only one player had made a switch under those rules. The NFLPA wanted unrestricted free agency for anyone who had been in the league four years.

We did have a list of issues we felt were important, such as a league-wide drug policy, roster-size changes, and some adjustments of the pension system. Free agency was way down on the list. Yet, we were solid as a union. We sent more representatives to the NFLPA convention in Los Angeles back in March than any team in the league. We had no players who refused to strike.

Art told the media, "I promise you there are at least 35 to 40 players on the Browns that if I told them they were a free agent, they'd pass out from fright. They don't want it."

Another big difference between the '82 strike and this one was we were making a whole lot more money, which meant we'd be losing a lot more money each week the strike dragged on. That would cost someone like Bernie Kosar $50,000 per week. Two quarterbacks—Marc Wilson of the Raiders and Gary Hogeboom of the Colts, feared striking could cost them hundreds of thousands of dollars in their guaranteed contracts, and thus they refused to strike. Complicating the issue further was the fact the owners had replacement players at the ready, which really hacked us off, as well as a $150 million line of credit to sustain them through the work stoppage. Strike or not, the season would continue. The strike date, approved by the players' association by a vote of 24-4 and originally kept secret, was September 22, after completion of Week 2 of the regular season.

I missed the activities from the first week of the strike as I was home in Theodore dealing with my mother's hospitalization. I watched stories of the strike on the news and talked to a couple of the guys. Mike Pagel was our new players' representative, and Matt Bahr was the alternate. Some fans showed up at Browns' headquarters in Berea, bringing coffee and doughnuts; others articulated their feelings on the strike with horn honks and thumbs up or their middle finger extended. Drivers of FedEx and UPS trucks refused to make pickups or deliveries at Browns headquarters at Baldwin-Wallace College. Steelworkers and other union members joined the guys on the picket line. The Ironworkers said they'd encircle the Stadium and make sure no one got in on Sunday. Altogether, some 20 unions joined the picket line.

Mike urged the team to avoid violence and threats. For the most part, the players complied, at least in Cleveland. Ray Ellis was most active of the dozen guys who showed up on the picket line Tuesday morning. He threw himself on the ground in front of a car that Red Man Redding was driving, although they both wound up laughing it off. The next day, Ray dumped a garbage bag full of pizza boxes and napkins on the hood of replacement quarterback Jeff Christensen's car. "If I ever get a shot at you, I'm going to take it," Ray yelled.

Eddie Johnson also got into the act, stopping Christensen's car by the Bagley Road parking lot exit and admonishing him that he wasn't doing the right thing. Eddie earned the title of "Most Menacing Picketer." By 10 a.m., the picketers either went home, went fishing, or played in a charity golf tournament at Kirtland Country Club. The goal was to convince about 25 of the 50 or so scabs to not cross, which would have made fielding a team next to impossible. But, did we really want to do that? If we succeeded in preventing the Browns from fielding a team, but the other teams didn't, then the Browns would have to forfeit those games, which would only put us deeper in a hole when the strike ended.

I can understand why the owners felt they had to keep the season going. They certainly were aware that the product on the field would be sub-par and would have only marginal fan support. But keeping the season going was critical, because if they shut the franchises down, that could be interpreted as a lockout and could create a whole new set of legal problems for them. On the other hand, I can't figure out just what would be the benefit of being a scab. Yes, they might make a little money here and now, but did they think for a second that this would enhance their chances of making it in the NFL later? Really, come on. What do you think would happen to a quarterback or a running back during the first contact scrimmages of camp? Do you think the offensive linemen would go out of their way to block for them? Fat chance. If they would honor the picket line, their chances of actually making the team at a later date would be significantly better.

In the locker room, the staff cleared out everything that belonged to us and placed it in garbage bags. The name plates above the lockers were taken down. Matt Bahr warned reporters not to cross the line and cover scab practices later in the week. Bubba Baker jogged along Bagley Road in Berea, saying that things were "ugly." But things got much uglier in other cities. A bus carrying replacement players in Houston was egged, and in Washington, a replacement players' bus had windows broken out. A pair of striking players in Kansas City showed up with rifles, yelling, "Where's the scabs?" Fortunately, the guns were unloaded. Steve Korte, center for the New Orleans Saints, crossed the line to get some treatment for an injury. He was labeled "nothing but a scab" by one of his teammates, Dave Waymer.

Meanwhile, Marty and the coaching staff had the very difficult job of putting together a team and preparing them for a game. He told us "Whatever you do, do it together." We all received letters from Art, who articulated his position and asked us to just be fully aware of what we are doing.

We were in a bit of a fix as to what to think of the "Tans"—the nickname ascribed to the replacement team by the media. While we certainly detested the idea of rooting for the scabs, it certainly would be to our benefit that they win. But that would weaken our negotiating position. If the scabs lost, that might pressure ownership to resolve the issue quicker, but it could put a severe crimp in our playoff chances.

Cracks in the players' ranks were evident early. An ESPN poll showed that only 25 percent of the fans favored the players' side, 73 percent favored the owners, and 2 percent were undecided. I'm sure the fans weren't too sympathetic to guys making an average of $16,000 per game. Matt Millen of the Raiders told Cable News Network, "We're striking for nothing." Gary Jeter of the Rams and Howie Long of the Raiders pointed out that National Football League Players' Association Executive Director Gene Upshaw was still getting paid during the strike, while the players weren't. "Gene Upshaw is not going to support my wife and son," Long surmised. Mark Gastineau of the Jets refused to strike.

*   *   *

On Sunday following the beginning of the strike, I sat in my mother's hospital room, trying to hold myself together. Mom sat up in bed and tapped what little strength she had left to talk to me.

"I'm just so tired," she said breathily. "Please don't worry about me. I know where I'm going, and soon I will be in a glorified state. God's calling for me. It's time for me to go. I love you, Hanford." I lost it. I was in pieces. No sweeter, more caring, stronger Christian woman ever walked this earth.

The games for Week 3 were cancelled, wiping out our *Monday Night Football* rematch with the Broncos at the Stadium. But as far as my life was concerned, it was divine intervention that that game was cancelled. At 10:15 p.m. that night, in what would have been in the middle of that *Monday Night Football* game, I stood beside my mother's bed along with my sister and her husband, my dad, and my mother's sister Elizabeth as my mother heard the call of God and returned to be with Him. Thank you, Lord, for this strike.

*   *   *

In Week 4, the first week of the replacement games, the Browns traveled to New England, a team that had five players who crossed the line, and a meager 14,830 fans showed up. But the Tans came from behind to win, 20-10.

In the second week of the strike, we began to hold team work-outs on our own, led by Gary Danielson. But across the league, more and more players broke ranks and came back. At a team meeting on Tuesday after the win over the Patriots, Carl Hairston, the oldest guy on the team, said he was crossing the line. Some guys were pissed at him, but Carl was one of the more respected guys on the team, and his honesty and frankness were appreciated. But even with Carl's help, the Tans lost to Houston, 15-10. The Oilers were probably hoping the strike would never end. They were now 3-1, sitting in first place, and off to their best start since 1979.

The pressure began to mount in the third week of the strike. More and more players across the league were crossing the line, and tensions were mounting within the Browns as well. Marty, who had previously urged us to do whatever we did together, backpedaled. He now said that each player needed to do what he felt was in his own best interest. Art made a similar statement.

At a very tense players meeting Tuesday night, the arguments and insults were flying. The team was divided three ways: the hard-core, stick-to-the-union guys; the guys in the middle who wanted to go along with the majority; and those who figured the whole strike was a waste. I was with the hardcore group. I despised the scabs and thought we should stay with the union all the way. Cody Risien and Brian Brennan bolted out of the meeting. They had had enough. The next day, they were joined by Sam Clancy, Jeff Gossett, and Jeff Jaeger. But the big surprise came later that afternoon when Ozzie Newsome and Gary Danielson reported for practice. Seven other guys on the injured reserve list also reported to practice in time to make the league cutoff date for those who wanted to participate in the upcoming weekend games. Across the league, 228 guys crossed the line.

The team was fractured, the unity gone, the union busted, and animosity was running high. Dave Puzzuoli said that "anyone who goes in is a pretty boy only thinking of himself." Frank was pissed off too, saying that the guys who crossed "are not our leaders. We can't depend on them when we need them most. We need to elect new captains on this team."

This was particularly distressful to me. I had just buried my mother, and now my two closest friends on the team, Frank and Ozzie were at very bitter odds.

But the battle was over. The strike that no one really wanted had failed. There would be no changes to free agency for now, nor would there be any change on any other issues of concern.

The strike of 1982 had at least produced some results, such as establishing a minimum salary schedule, increase training camp and postseason pay, increasing medical and retirement benefits, and introducing a severance pay system. No such improvements this time around, at least for now.

On Thursday, NFLPA President Gene Upshaw ran up the white flag and ordered everyone back to work. But that was a day past the deadline to play that weekend, so the replacement players, along with the veterans who had crossed over, would play one more game. The Browns had another big divisional game, this one in Cincinnati, but it was definitely advantage Browns. Only two Bengals had crossed the line, and the Browns had their regulars back in nine key positions. Paul Brown whined that it wasn't a fair fight, and he was right. The Browns whomped the Bengals, 34-0, and regained a tie with Houston for first place as the Oilers lost to New England.

*   *   *

The strike now being over, we needed to get back to business. We were all a bit nervous as to what to expect when we all got together at practice at Browns headquarters on the campus of Baldwin-Wallace College in Berea. We knew, though, that the difficulties of the strike had to be put behind us and fast. Holding grudges against each other would serve no purpose. What was done was done. The scab team did us a favor by winning two of three games, and we were in position for another great run.

Rain drizzled from the gray Cleveland sky, and we cautiously went about our usual practice routines. Everyone was a bit on edge, but the rainy weather gave me a spontaneous idea. I began to sing the theme to *Gilligan's Island*. Everyone looked at me like I was weird, and maybe they were right, but as I sang it, others began to join in. Pretty soon just about everyone was singing along, and you could feel the tensions ease. I don't think my tale of a fateful trip brought us together—that was going to happen anyway. It was just the catalyst.

We re-booted the season on a Monday night game against the Rams. Eric Dickerson was whining for a better contract or to be traded, and the Rams stumbled out to a 1-4 start. That meant old friend Charles White was going to give it a go. But it was no contest. We jumped off to a 17-0 lead, and before you knew it, it was 30-7. We cruised to a 30-17 win, and the chemistry was flowing again. Nothing heals rifts like winning.

We went on to win six of the remaining nine games, including two tough road games at the end of the regular season. We traveled to Los Angeles, beating the Raiders 24-17, and then went to Pittsburgh and beat the goddamn Steelers 19-13. Our defense did a number on those goddamn Steelers, holding them to a grand total of one offensive play in the fourth quarter, where I picked off Mark Malone at midfield. But it was the front office that kept the stars properly aligned from the win we had in Three Rivers the previous year. Art made sure the seating arrangements in his box were the same. Ernie Accorsi wore the same socks. Eleven penalties on the goddamn Steelers didn't hurt things, either. We finished 10-5 and were division champions again. We got a week off and then faced the 9-6 Eastern Division champion Indianapolis Colts in the divisional playoff.

Under new head coach Ron Meyer, the Colts were enjoying the fruits of a quick-turnaround team. They were 3-13 the year before after starting off 0-13. Rod Dowhower was fired, and Meyer took over. Instead of just going through the motions for the final three meaningless games, the Colts set the tone for the next season by winning the last three games. The Colts beat us, 9-7, at home just a month before in a game where our offense just took the day off. We kept Eric Dickerson, acquired from the Rams in an October trade, in check, holding him under 100 yards and recovering a fumble. In what would be a hauntingly prophetic moment, Earnest Byner fumbled the ball inside the Colts' 5 in the fourth quarter, costing us the chance to take the lead. So we knew we could hold them on defense, and if our offense could get it together, our chances would be pretty good.

The field was iced up as one would expect for a January afternoon on the lakefront. The grounds crew probably should have used a Zamboni to prepare the field. We were ready for this game, but we were somewhat subdued. Getting to the playoffs was not our goal—winning the Super Bowl was. We knew we could beat these guys and fully expected to.

We had already lost Bob Golic for the rest of the season with a broken arm in the Pittsburgh game. Kevin Mack went down with a stomach virus, and guard Larry Williams hurt his ankle in the first half, and a 19-yard pass from Jack Trudeau to Dickerson tied the score, 14-14, at the half. The fans booed us as we came off the field. In the locker room, Eddie Johnson let us have it.

"What the fuck is the matter with you assholes?" he bellowed at us. "We should have shut their fucking asses down. We know we're better than this, and better than them." We sat there quietly, knowing that he was right. And it would be Eddie who would spark us in the first drive of the second half, giving us control of the game.

We re-installed the hybrid-Bears defense for this game. The Colts took the second-half kickoff and, utilizing a lot of dump-off passes to Dickerson and Albert Bentley, marched down to our 20 in 11 plays. That's when Eddie stepped up huge for us. He blitzed through on the next play and got to Trudeau, who tossed up an ill-advised desperation pass, which wobbled into the hands of safety Felix Wright at our 14. From there, Bernie and the gang drove 86 yards for the go-ahead score, with Earnest Byner going in from the 2. The momentum and control were now ours, and the game was mostly fun from that point. Matt Bahr kicked a 22-yard field goal, Bernie hit Brian Brennan for another score, and Frank Minnifield closed things out with a 48-yard interception return. Final score: Browns 38, Colts 21.

After the game, we were pleased, yes, and let out a few barks in the locker room, but overall, we were rather reserved. This was a game we fully expected to win, and we did, but we knew the job wasn't close to being done. Only a Super Bowl victory would suffice.

The Oilers were playing the Broncos in the other AFC divisional game, and if Oilers would pull off the upset, they would come to the Stadium for the AFC title game. If the Broncos won, we would have to go to Denver to take on the Broncos in the rematch of last year's title game. The Broncos defeated the Oilers, 34-10, so it was off to Denver.

For only the third time in history, the AFC title game would be a rematch of the previous year's game. We certainly had revenge on our minds. As dramatic and heart-wrenching as the title game from the 1986 season was, no one could have anticipated what was going to unfold this season at the base of the Rockies. We were ready with our hybrid-Bears defense, and Earnest Byner was healthy. The Broncos featured John Elway and his "Three Amigos"—wide receivers Vance Johnson, Ricky Nattiel, and Mark Jackson. Johnson was out due to a groin injury suffered in the playoff win over Houston, and three Broncos starters had retired from the previous year, but their offense was still plenty potent.

Very much like the previous year, Browns mania swept the city. A replica of a 150 million-year-old stegosaurus donned a Browns hat and gloves in the Cleveland Museum of Natural History. Big-screen TVs were hot rental items. The homicide units of the Cleveland and Denver police departments wagered a collection of baseball caps. An up-and-coming politician named Al Gore, Jr., gave a speech in town, sporting a Browns button. Keeping things bipartisan, President Ronald Reagan delivered a speech to the City Club of Cleveland, where he was handed a sweatshirt proclaiming, "Go Browns! Win One for the Gipper!"

Two big announcements were overshadowed by the week's hysteria. These were two decisions that would shape the future of Browns history. Forrest Gregg resigned as Green Bay's head coach to take over duties of his alma mater, Southern Methodist University, which was left in shambles after crushing NCAA sanctions. That paved the way for our offensive coordinator, Lindy Infante, to take over in Green Bay. The day after that news came, St. Louis owner William Bidwell announced the Cardinals were moving to Phoenix. Bidwell turned down offers from Jacksonville, Memphis, and Baltimore. This left Baltimore, which lost the Colts to Indianapolis in a 1984 midnight move, desperate for a franchise, making that city ripe for a replacement team, and we all know too well what happened in 1995.

*   *   *

Denver was certainly a tough town in which to play. Maybe it's the altitude, maybe it's just our attitude. Since Dan Reeves took over as head coach in 1981, Denver was 42-11 at home. They had won all their non-strike home games. We, on the other hand, had lost four straight at Mile High Stadium and hadn't won there in 15 years. The weather was bright and sunny, the temperature moderate, so weather, unfortunately, was not a factor in the game. As we warmed up on the field, highlights of "The Drive" were played ad nauseam. To add a little dig, we also watch Shane Conlan of Buffalo, the guy we passed on to get Mike Junkin, collect the NFL Rookie of the Year Award.

Trouble came early and often for our offense. On the first series, a pass from Bernie to Webster Slaughter slipped out of his hands and into the clutches of defensive end Freddie Gilbert at our 18. Elway then hit Nattiel for a touchdown three plays later. After we got the ball back, Kevin Mack lost the ball to safety Tony Lilly, setting up the Broncos at their 40. Gene Lang then ripped through us to the 11, and Frank got flagged for a holding penalty which gave the Broncos a first down on our 2. Steve Sewell took it in on a reverse, and before we could break a sweat we were down, 14-0.

We got a field goal on our next possession, but Mike Baab twisted his knee and was out for the rest of the game. Larry Williams, who was already gimpy, came in at left guard, and Gregg Rakoczy moved over to center.

Denver then drove right down on us again, with Lang taking it in from the 1. We countered with a missed field goal, and were now in a deep hole, 21-3. Most teams would have folded it up and made their golf reservations. In the locker room at halftime, there was no panic, no finger-pointing, no name-calling. Lindy told the offense we were going to play the game "like it was 14-7." No change in the game plan, no two-minute offense. Marty told those of us on defense to just keep our heads clear and play like we were capable of playing.

We started on defense in the third quarter, and Felix Wright came up with a big interception, which he returned to the Denver 35. Bernie later hit Reggie Langhorne for an 18-yard score, and it was now 21-10. Elway then hit Jackson on an 80-yard catch-and-run down the sideline, and for a good number of us and our fans, the party was over. But not for Earnest Byner. Earnest would spearhead one of the greatest comebacks ever, only to meet a most cruel fate as he was about to be canonized.

Earnest came from Milledgeville, Georgia, where his high school team won four games in three years. Herschel Walker was the big draw among scouts those years, and Earnest was lucky to make it to East Carolina University. The Browns drafted him in the 10th round in 1984, only after noticing him on film while examining another player. What a steal he turned out to be. He started out in the insane world of special teams, but Marty realized Earnest was more than just a part-timer.

"In my mind," Marty told *The Plain Dealer*, "Byner possesses the quality you find inside people which lets them accomplish things beyond their natural skills."

Earnest's heroics began in the third quarter. He snagged a looping pass from Bernie and, taking advantage of a big block by Kevin Mack, bolted to pay dirt 33 yards away. That made it 28-17, still a steep hill to climb in the toughest NFL stadium for a road team to win, but the momentum had swung back our way. On defense we held, and after Gerald McNeil's punt return, our offense was set up at Denver's 42. Bernie and the boys wasted no time. After completions to Webster and Kevin, Earnest took it in from the 4. Just like that, it was 28-24, with still over three minutes to go in the third quarter. Rich Karlis barefooted a 38-yard field goal to put the Broncos up, 31-24, as we began what would be an epic fourth quarter. A fourth quarter that would bring out the best in Earnest Byner, but so sadly everyone remembers him for what happened at the end.

Bernie lobbed a pass to Earnest on a big third-and-5 from our 19. He zipped 53 yards, setting up a 5-yard strike from Bernie to

Webster. Now the score was 31-31, and there were more than 10 minutes to go.

After an exchange of punts, the Broncos drove down, and Elway hit Sammy Winder on a 20-yard screen play for the go-ahead score. With 3:53 to go, Bernie and the boys methodically drove downfield, with Earnest ripping off 17 yards on the first play. After a big completion to Brian Brennan for 20 yards, Earnest picked up 6 yards on a 13-trap play, giving us a first down on the Denver 13. After a couple of incompletions and an offside call against the Broncos, we were perched at the 8, second-and-5, with 1:12 remaining. The call came in. Again, it was 13 trap. Browns fans agonizingly remember the details. So do I. I stood there on the sideline, just as helpless to do anything about it as Browns fans were watching on television around the world. Earnest took the ball and headed for the end zone. It sure looked like he made it, and we were waiting for the official to raise his hands to signal touchdown. In anticipation, we jumped for joy. But by the time our feet hit the ground, we were in apoplectic shock. Earnest was in the end zone, yes, but the ball was on the 2, and Denver's Jeremiah Castille was on top of it. Goddammit, which is a mild term compared to what was yelled and screamed on our sideline.

Earnest lay on his side in the end zone, racked by a most unbelievable pain. I never experienced anything like that in my career, and it was so sad to see such a great man writhe in such mental anguish.

What made this even more tragic is that it wiped Earnest's herculean performance to get us to that place and time. All of his career, and especially this game, Earnest played his heart out. Earnest was one of the toughest, hardest-working guys ever to play this thing called pro football. He was the last guy on Earth who deserved such a terrible fate.

Earnest trudged to the sideline and sat down on his helmet. Brian, Bernie, and a few others tried to console him, which he acknowledged as graciously as a sorrowful man could. This class man and athlete accounted for 187 yards of offense, but it all counted for nothing. Just what could one say to him? Sorry? Get 'em next time? Keep your head up? There are no words that would have fit. Nonetheless, I looked him in the eye and said, "Never, ever, are you to blame yourself for this. We win as a team and lose as a team. You played your guts out, and none of us would have gotten this far without you." Earnest was as gracious as anyone possibly could be in this situation, but his pain was still obvious. Probably everyone on the team told him the same thing I did.

As the media surrounded Earnest in the locker room, he stood there and answered all of the questions. He didn't duck the issues or blame anyone or anything else. Usually in a situation like that, the player takes a real quick shower and inconspicuously ducks out of the locker room before the media are let in. Not Earnest. He faced the music with class and style. I probably would have uttered obscenities every other word and slammed a few helmets around just for effect. The fans and media were good to Earnest—no one blamed him for the loss. In fact, everyone was in agreement that if it weren't for Earnest's big-time playmaking we wouldn't have been in a position to win or at least force overtime.

"Byner symbolizes that great fighting spirit," radio host Pete Franklin wrote. "He is the guy who refuses to give up, who keeps on battling the opponent."

Similar accolades came from *Plain Dealer* sports columnist Doug Clarke. "There was something very Cleveland-like in the way Byner, knowing he already had the first down, strove to make it in the end zone," he wrote. "Disappointed, yes; bitter and angry, no. How do you get mad at a team that refused to quit and provided us with one of the most thrilling of championship games in the history of the NFL?"

Two years later, in one of the all-time bad trades, the Browns sent Earnest to the Redskins for Mike Oliphant. Mike had two un-eventful years with the Browns before being exiled to Sacramento of the Canadian Football League, while Earnest prospered in Washington. With the Redskins, he made it to Super Bowl XXVI, where he caught a touchdown pass in the second quarter of the Redskins' 37-24 victory over Buffalo. He was selected for the Pro Bowl in 1990. The Browns re-signed him in 1994, and he played the final two seasons in Cleveland before the Browns moved to Baltimore. He continued his career with the Ravens, retiring in 1997, and is 16th on the all-time rushers' list. He became the first Raven to be enshrined on the Ravens' Ring of Honor in 2001. He is now the running backs coach for the Jacksonville Jaguars.

In 2011, the Jaguars played a game in Cleveland, and a sideline shot of Earnest was put up on the big screen at Browns Stadium. The crowd roared its appreciation for the great athlete and human being he always was and always will be.

CHAPTER FOURTEEN

Riverboat Sam, Martyball, and Bud

Over my nine seasons with the Browns, I worked under three head coaches. Each had his own distinct way of doing things. All three were brilliant football minds. All three brought great hopes of restoring the great winning tradition of the Cleveland Browns. All three left under very difficult circumstances.

Sam Rutigliano was the head coach when I arrived in Cleveland. A truly funny guy who had seen great triumphs and tragedies. He was born to immigrant parents on July 1, 1933, in Sheepshead Bay, New York, the same Brooklyn neighborhood that produced former Green Bay Packers coach Vince Lombardi and former Penn State coach Joe Paterno. He was a star wide receiver in high school and subsequently at Tennessee and Tulsa. After coaching high school ball, Sam ascended to the college ranks, coaching at the University of Connecticut, the University of Maryland, and the University of Tennessee.

He then joined the Denver Broncos' staff as an assistant and, as assistant coaches often do, coached several other teams over 11 years. He spent time with the Jets, the Patriots and the Saints. While mired in another losing season for Saints in 1977, Sam got a call from Browns director of football operations Peter Hadhazy. Hadhazy told Sam that they were about to give Forrest Gregg the ax, and that—very likely—the job would be his if he just didn't blow the interview. Art Modell was also interested in Paterno, Ara Parseghian, and Joe Restic, but Sam was the man. After the final game of the 1977 regular season, Sam had dinner with Art Modell. They spent the next day at Art's house, talking football, looking at film. Sam left feeling confident the job was his, and on Christmas Eve 1977, Art called and made the offer to Sam. He became the first head coach of the Browns who wasn't promoted from within the system.

Here's a sad fact that most people don't know about Sam: In 1962, while driving from Montreal to Maine, Sam fell asleep at the wheel and rolled his Volkswagen. The accident took the life of his 4-year-old daughter, Nancy. Can you imagine the heartache and guilt he must have carried for years?

I first met Sam and Marty Schottenheimer, his defensive coordinator, at the Senior Bowl in Mobile, Alabama. They were interested in me, and I was interested in them. I was glad to have been picked by the Browns in the 1981 draft and looked forward to a great career with them.

It was the spring of 1982 when Rich Kotite, the receivers coach, walked in to Sam's office and closed the door. He told Sam there was a drug problem on the team, a big drug problem. At first, Sam didn't want to believe it. But later Sam relayed the news to Art Modell, who asked Sam what action they should take. Instead of simply demanding that anybody who uses drugs just be shown the door, Sam asked Art to fund a formal, organized program to deal with the problem, treating it like a disease. This is how the Inner Circle was formed. Players could anonymously get first-class treatment at the Cleveland Clinic, fully funded by Art Modell. This clearly became the hallmark of Sam's career with the Browns. It served as a model for other teams as well. There is no telling just how many careers—and lives—were saved.

Sam had other issues to deal with as well. Early in the 1982 season, Sam's 16-year-old daughter, Kerry, attempted suicide by cutting her wrists. She also suffered from bulimia. But that was the year of the strike, and fortunately for Sam and his family, the trouble with Kerry came on just as the strike did, allowing Sam more time to tend to the very critical issues at home.

Having taught high school in Brooklyn, Sam knew how to handle guys who thought they were tough shit. That gave him great training and insight on how to handle kids who came to town thinking they're hot shit, like me.

In Sam's first year of teaching, one particularly obnoxious kid stood up in homeroom and flung the f-bomb in Sam's face. Sam decked the kid. Feeling awful about it, Sam reported the incident to the principal, who contacted the boy's father. At the conference in the principal's office, the boy's father shook Sam's hand and told his punkass kid that "when you're at dis school, he's da boss, see? You do what he says, see? If you don't, I'll give you more to worry about dan he has, see?" Problem solved. That's the way things were done in those days, and sadly, that's what we're missing now. If Sam had done that nowadays, damn, could you imagine the lawsuits that would be flying around?

I have always been a high-strung, emotional player. I knew the game, and I knew I was good. Yes, I was cocky, and I really didn't like it when others, no matter how experienced or wise, told me what to do. Sam saw this in me, and instead of slugging me, which he probably should have done a few dozen times, he turned that attitude around back at me. He would challenge me, to the point of insulting me. I would constantly hear him say, even after I thought I made a good play, "Hanford, what's your problem? You're much better than that." He wasn't interested in using pop psychology or rah-rah motivational speeches. To this day, he maintains that I was a major pain in the ass. I'm sure I was. I know I was. But that's the way I am, and Sam's the way Sam is.

Not long ago, we were signing autographs at an event, and Sam walked over to me, quipping, "Look. There's your problem. You keep misspelling your name."

Sam earned the nickname "Riverboat Sam" for his on-field

gambles in critical situations, such as going for it on fourth down when conventional wisdom dictated punting. Some of the gambles worked out well, but then there was Red Right 88 and a few other incidents that overshadowed the successes. After his final game, losing a 12-9 field-goal fest in Cincinnati, Sam was still determined to carry on, even though he was well aware of all the heat being applied. He declared to the media after the game, "I will be here for the next game and for the remainder of the season."

After being fired in the middle of the horrible 1984 season, he was considered for coaching positions with Buffalo, as well as Northwestern University, the University of Maryland, and Louisiana State University. But he signed on with NBC and had his own pregame show on ESPN. He did the broadcast circuit for five years. Then he got a call from Liberty University in Lynchburg, Virginia, the university founded and headed by Jerry Falwell, leader of the Moral Majority. It was actually a good fit for Sam, who is a deeply spiritual man.

He had to overcome some rather major recruiting obstacles to build the program at Liberty University. They had very, very strict moral conduct codes, so strict that most guys would likely play college elsewhere. No smoking, drinking, engaging in sex, staying out past curfew, skipping chapel, not wearing ties, entering a women's dorm, watching R-rated movies, or having a TV in your dorm room. Despite that, Sam became the winningest coach in school history, and after "retiring" from Liberty in 2000, he unretired two hours later, taking the job as coach of the Barcelona Dragons of the NFL Europe league. He also coached the Glasgow Tigers and Hamburg Sea Devils. Sam loved it—he couldn't believe that they were paying him, too.

Like many former Browns players and coaches, Sam has maintained his home in Cleveland and is a staple of the community. After 57 years of marriage, he remains deeply in love and devoted to his wife Barbara, a nurse whom Sam met at a hospital after being in an auto accident. During his career, he moved 19 times and sold

13 houses, and had four kids. Barbara should have been given a Nobel Prize for putting up with that. Sam likes to talk about how through the years "divorce was never an option. It just wasn't. Murder, maybe, but never divorce! I mean she would have killed me, not the other way around."

New York Daily columnist Dick Young once called Sam "the luckiest Italian since Christopher Columbus." But Sam was a lot more than luck. He was the combination of a brilliant mind, strong character, toughness, and compassion. He and Paul Brown are the only Browns coaches to be named NFL Coach of the Year. He took my shit, turning it around on me to make me better, but never dished any out. He treated us as individuals, with our unique or odd personalities, strengths, and weaknesses.

But don't think for a second that Sam's pleasant demeanor was some sort of weakness. Art Modell said of Sam, "Those who mistake Sam's communication abilities and pleasant manner for softness do not last with the Browns. He's demanding and one of the most competitive persons I have ever met."

As Brian Sipe lay on the frozen turf after tossing the infamous Red Right 88 interception against the Raiders in 1981, Sam ran onto the field and helped up his fallen field general.

"Brian, I love you," he said, cradling the cold and exhausted quarterback's head, to which Brian replied, according to Sam, "I want a divorce."

It was very sad to see Sam get the ax. But I understand why. Things were spiraling downward, and something had to be done. The head coach is the easiest and most convenient scapegoat, and Sam found himself in that unenviable position.

Then it was Marty's turn.

*   *   *

Marty Schottenheimer was just a month past his 41st birthday when he took over head coaching duties. He came from Canonsburg, Pennsylvania, and played linebacker for the University of Pittsburgh. He was drafted in both the NFL and AFL Drafts by Baltimore (fourth round) and Buffalo (seventh round). He opted to sign with the Bills, where he played for four seasons. He had a stellar rookie season, making the AFL All-Star Team and being part of the Bills' AFL championship team the year before the Super Bowl. He jumped to the Boston Patriots for his last two seasons as a player. In 1971, he was traded to the goddamn Steelers and subsequently the Baltimore Colts before retiring from football for the real estate industry in Miami and Denver, a career path I similarly followed in Cleveland.

While working as a developer in Denver, Marty visited with Joe Collier, the Broncos' defensive coordinator, who had coached Marty during his days in Buffalo. Marty wanted to learn the coaching business and subsequently joined the staff of the World Football League's Portland Storm, originally to be a player-coach, but a shoulder injury facilitated his efforts to be focused on coaching. He also served as an assistant coach for the New York Giants and Detroit Lions before Sam brought him to Cleveland to be the Browns' defensive coordinator in 1980.

We finished 4-4 in the second half of the 1984 season under Marty, not bad at all considering three of those losses (Pittsburgh, Cincinnati, New Orleans) came on final-play field goals. Indicative of the weird goings-on in 1984, Charles White had to be put on the injured reserve list because of back spasms. That might not sound too weird, but he suffered those back spasms during a team meeting. Go figure. I finished the year with 61 tackles, 45 of them solo, and 22 passes defended—tops on the team for three years. I snagged two of my five interceptions at Three Rivers. Four of my five interceptions set up scores.

One thing you knew about Marty is that he was very emotional. We would take bets among ourselves as to when he was going to cry. In the midst of a team meeting, a pre- or postgame speech, or just yelling at a guy who screwed up, you never knew when Marty's eyes, behind those bug-eyed glasses, would start to moisten. Usually teams break into groups (linemen, backs, linebackers, etc.) to watch game film, but Marty made us all watch game film on Mondays together. During one meeting, Marty called me out on a play.

"Hanford, you can't play it this way," he said. "You've got to play it the way we're showing you."

That didn't sit too well with me. No one likes to be called out in front of everybody. Especially those who know it all, like me.

"Let me tell you something," I snapped. "I played it just fine, and it worked just fucking fine. And I'll play it that way the fucking next time as well."

The room went silent. No one moved a muscle or drew a breath. You could have heard a rat piss on a cotton ball. Marty stood there stoically, his steely eyes slowly bulging through the frames of his giant spectacles. Gritting his teeth, he slowly declared, "This meeting is now over. For everyone except Hanford Dixon."

Everyone quickly gathered up their notebooks and belongings and scrambled away like townspeople fleeing down the dusty road as the Goon brothers were staring down the sheriff of Dodge City. Marty and I proceeded to his office, and we let it rip. We argued, yelled, and exchanged obscenities, calling each other more names than any two gifted 4-year-olds could imagine. But after about an hour, we effectively wore each other out. We agreed we had a job to do, and we were going to get it done. We hugged and went on our way. That's the type of relationship Marty and I had.

I recall during one meeting Judson Flint did the unspeakable—he dozed off. Marty, still defensive coordinator at the time, saw Judson snoozing and yelled, "Judson! Wake up!"

Somewhat startled, Judson uttered, "My eyes wasn't closed."

"Oh yes, they were!" Marty snapped.

"My eyes wasn't closed."

"Oh yes, they were!"

They went back and forth a few times before Judson finally realized the best strategy was to shut up.

It was open season on our quarterbacks in 1988, with our starters getting injured five times. Bernie Kosar went down with an
elbow injury in Week 1, then Gary Danielson broke his left ankle
in Week 2, then four games later, Mike Pagel went down with a
separated shoulder while making a touchdown-saving tackle on a
blocked field-goal return in a loss to Seattle. We were still in the
playoff run, so we obviously needed a veteran quarterback—now.
The Browns found Don Strock, who was 38 years old, had left the
Miami Dolphins in a contract dispute, and was living the good life
as a celebrity greeter at the Doral County Club in south Florida.
His agent had the Browns by the balls in contract negotiations,
but nonetheless, the deal got done. We were 3-3, and the season
now hinged on this tanned and paunchy dude who hadn't started
a game in five years.

Don strapped a chart of 55 plays on his left wrist and proceeded
to lead us to a 19-3 win over the Philadelphia Eagles at the old stadium, tossing a pair of touchdowns to Reggie Langhorne and Webster Slaughter. Our defense simply stuffed Randall Cunningham,
sacking him nine times. He had been the NFC Offensive Player of
the Week just the week before. But it should have been a shutout.
Their tight end, Keith Jackson, went after my fucking throat, and
in self-defense, I fucking fought back. But of course, I was the one
who got flagged. The refs rarely see the instigation, but they almost
always get you for the retaliation. Five plays later, the Eagles kicked
a field goal for their only measly points.

Our last two games of the 1988 season were against the Oilers.
We beat Houston in a snowy comeback on the lakefront, a game I
missed with a bad groin, setting up a wild-card playoff game the
next week at home. The Oilers came back and beat us, 24-23, to end
our season.

Art called Marty in for a meeting on December 26. He wanted
Marty to bring on an offensive coordinator and reassign his brother
Kurt, who was special teams coach. No final decision was reached
in that meeting, and Marty headed back to his office. There he

picked up *The Plain Dealer*, and the headline leached from the page right to his soul.

"Modell won't let coaches stand pat."

Art already had made known his plans via the media. The meeting with Marty was only perfunctory. I can understand how this pissed Marty off to no end. He picked up the phone and called Ernie Accorsi, the director of football operations.

"It's over," Marty said. It was just that simple. He compiled a record of 44-27 with the Browns, with four playoff appearances, three AFC Central Division titles, and two trips to the AFC Championship Game. No Browns coach has had a winning record since.

Marty soon thereafter went on to coach Kansas City for 10 years and brought the Chiefs back to Cleveland for a game that resulted in a 10-10 tie. He resigned in 1999 after a disappointing 7-9 season. He worked as an analyst for ESPN for two years, then signed on as head coach of the Washington Redskins. There, he had to contend with "boy genius" (gag) owner Daniel Snyder. The Redskins lost their first five games but then became the first team in NFL history to also then win their next five games. They won eight of their final 11 games and just missed the playoffs. Despite the great second-half comeback, Snyder gave Marty the boot after just one season, thinking he had a big winner in former University of Florida coach Steve Spurrier.

Marty went on the coach the San Diego Chargers, racking up a record of 47-33, with two playoff appearances. Spurrier led the Redskins to a 12-20 record over the next two seasons, doing no better than 7-9 in 2002.

But Marty's nepotistic tendencies got him in trouble in San Diego. His son Brian was the quarterbacks coach, and he wanted his brother Kurt to replace Wade Phillips as defensive coordinator. Chargers owner Dean Spanos opposed the move, but Marty defied his boss and booked his brother on a flight to San Diego anyway. Marty also was at odds with General Manager A.J. Smith, who was ticked off that four of Marty's assistants were leaving the staff after the 2006 season, despite the club's 14-2 regular-season record. On February 12, 2007, Marty was given the boot and replaced by Norv Turner, who ironically was the last full-time head coach before Marty's short stint with Washington. The Chargers then started off the following season 1-3, and their fans began choruses of "Marty! Marty! Marty!" in protest.

Marty was then hired by the Virginia Destroyers of the United Football League in March 2011. The Destroyers beat the two-time defending champion Las Vegas Locos, 17-3, in October 2011, giving 68-year-old Marty his first coaching championship.

Marty was a coach's coach. Bill Cowher, Gunther Cunningham, Tony Dungy, Lindy Infante, Mike McCarthy, Herman Edwards, Cam Cameron, Wade Phillips, and Tony Sparano all coached under his leadership, becoming head coaches themselves. Marty himself became the first coach in the modern era to head up four NFL teams.

A Marty Schottenheimer team was always prepared. Marty prided himself in knowing what the opposition was going to do. We had our spats, but we also cared about each other deeply. In 1987, I wrote a "guest" article for *The Plain Dealer* and stated that Marty should have been Coach of the Year. I still feel that way.

*   *   *

On January 27, 1989, the Browns, preparing for their 40th season, hired their seventh head coach, Leon "Bud" Carson. Others considered for the position included Minnesota's Floyd Peters, Chicago's Vince Tobin, Fritz Shurmur of the Rams, as well as this up-and-coming young assistant in the Giants organization named Bill Belichick. George Seifert, who was an assistant for the 49ers, fresh off a Super Bowl win over the Bengals, was actually on his way to Cleveland to meet with Art about the job, but during a layover in Dallas, he was paged by 49ers owner Eddie DeBartolo, Jr., and told to hurry back to San Francisco. Bill Walsh had just retired, and DeBartolo wanted Seifert to take over head coaching duties there.

There were a lot of odd similarities between Bud and Blanton Collier. They had the same initials. They were the same age when the Browns hired them. Both had sub-par records as college coaches, and both wore hearing aids.

Bud starting coaching in 1955, leading Scottsdale High School, just outside Pittsburgh, to a record of 16-2-1 over two seasons. Pretty damn good for a team that fielded only 18 players. He was the head coach at Georgia Tech from 1967 to '71, replacing the legendary Bobby Dodd. From 1972 to '77 Bud was the architect of the "Steel Curtain" in Pittsburgh, and after also serving as defensive coordinator for five NFL teams, he had 33 years of coaching experience. While with the Los Angeles Rams, Bud's defense set an NFL record by holding the Seattle Seahawks to minus-26 yards total offense.

We had the best record in the AFC over the past three years and had been in the playoffs four straight seasons, also best in the AFC. We were at the top of our game and certainly couldn't afford to take a step back. Our team was aging and our division improving. Bud, who served 30 months in the Marine Corps, put together a fine staff, mostly from the Jets' organization, with five assistants having coached in 12 Super Bowls. Bud's teams had made the playoffs 11 times, and won two Super Bowls in three appearances. In contrast, Sam's record as an assistant before coming to the Browns was 46-92-2, never having been part of a winning team.

So Bud's résumé and experience were in fine order. He knew the game inside and out, and had a fine product with which to work. Not everyone was impressed, though. Bernie Kosar was on a golf course in Florida when he heard the news that Bud was the new coach. "I threw for over 400 yards against his defense," Bernie said. "Why are we hiring him?" And there was the ill-fated experiment with switching me to safety, but we got past that. There were some stipulations of the job, too, which seemed a bit unreasonable. First, Bud was to have little to nothing to do with the upcoming draft. Art believed the scouting department was best suited for making those decisions and was smarting from a lengthy list of recent years' draft-day couldn't-miss misses. Also, Art had hired 33-year-old Marc Trestman as offensive coordinator, and the new head coach, whomever that would be, would have to go along with that appointment. Most of the previous assistant coaches followed Marty to Kansas City. Wide receivers coach Richard Mann and strength coach Dave Redding were the only holdovers from Marty's staff.

Art uttered those infamous words: "This is it for me. I've conducted my last coaching search."

All went well the first season, especially the opening game, when we destroyed the goddamn Steelers, 51-0, at Three Rivers. Big wins over Minnesota and Houston the last two weeks of the year gave us the division title by one-half game over Pittsburgh and Houston. But after the harrowing win over Buffalo in the divisional playoff, we lost to Denver in the title game.

There was something going on with Bud. He had been a lifelong smoker and had trouble getting himself to practice on time. He had to have Joe Popp, his assistant, pick him up daily and drag him around. But 1990 came along (I had retired before the season), and the bottom just fell out for Bud and the Browns.

The Browns got off to a good start, knocking off the goddamn Steelers, 13-3, in the opener at the Stadium, but then proceeded to lose seven of the next eight, including shutouts of 34-0 to Marty's Kansas City Chiefs and 42-0 against Buffalo, the worst home loss in Browns history.

To no one's surprise, Bud was given his walking papers, serving the shortest term of any Browns permanent head coach.

Jim Shofner took over. The 1958 first-round draft choice for the Browns—the draft that brought the likes of Chuck Howley, Alex Karras, Jim Taylor, Ray Nitschke, John Madden, and Jerry Kramer into the league, the last four the Browns passed on—didn't fare any better. The Browns went 1-6 the rest of the way, including crushing defeats at the hands of the Oilers, 58-14, and 35-0 by the goddamn Steelers. In the five divisional games the Browns lost, they were outscored, 183-64. Bud saw what was coming. His house was put up for sale weeks before the ax fell.

"Coaching here is a tough job," Bud told the media. "Your hands are somewhat tied. The coach of the Browns doesn't have much power." Those and a few other remarks got Bud in trouble, supposedly violating a "no negative comment" clause in his contract. The Browns threatened to not pay him the balance due on his contract but eventually backed off. Bud claimed his remarks had been spoken off the record.

Meanwhile, Marty went on to enjoy an 11-5 record with the Chiefs and a wild-card playoff appearance.

For some reason, head coaching just wasn't the thing for Bud. But it could be argued that 1990 was an aberration for him. Mike Ditka, Don Shula, Chuck Noll, and Tom Landry all went through lean years, and they all turned out pretty well. "Bud didn't get a fair shake at all," Raymond Clayborn told *The Plain Dealer*. Felix Wright added, "I will never understand how Bud was treated." He had had plenty of success prior, having led us to the AFC title game just the previous season, and he continued his successes after returning to the ranks of defensive coordinator for the Eagles and the Rams. The 1991 Eagles were ranked first against the pass and first against the run, and first in overall defense.

I'm sure it's a good thing that the players on the 1990 squad were loyal to Bud. In my last season, his first as head coach, Bud was loyal to his men, especially his defense, with one exception: me. I still don't understand why he squeezed me off the Browns the way he did, and informed me of his actions and decision through the media.

Bud retired in 1997 due to health reasons. Sadly, he died in Florida in 2005 of emphysema.

CHAPTER FIFTEEN

Favorite Game #4: Browns vs. Bills, Jan. 6, 1990

Clay Matthews could afford pretty much any car he wanted after 11 seasons in the NFL. But he always drove a beater. It seemed to fit him just fine, and he didn't seem impressed by the flashy rides the rest of us zipped around town in. Clay would show up in a '67 Camaro, a '66 Mustang, a '63 Mustang, or a rusted, brown '73 Mercury Capri—a two-door coupe that seemed to be his favorite. Being a pretty big guy, it was funny to watch Clay shoehorn himself into that sardine can.

Clay was as focused and as reliable as the sunrise. He joked and screwed around with the rest of us, like driving little remote control cars around the practice facility, but he always did his homework. He never had to be told to do anything twice. When no one knew the answer to a tough question in a team meeting, Clay would come up with it. He always wanted to be on the field for as many things as possible during practice. That meant he would play on the scout team, which regulars rarely did. He also would play fullback or even quarterback against our second-team defense.

Drafted along with Ozzie Newsome in the first round of the 1978 draft, California Clay and his long golden-brown locks of Sampson-like hair had been through the battles. He took over starting linebacker duties from Gerald Irons in 1979. He was the only linebacker on the squad to play every defensive down in 1989. He had football genes—his dad played four seasons with San Francisco in the 1950s, and his brother, Bruce, played 16 seasons with the Oilers. His son now terrorizes quarterbacks and runners in Green Bay. Clay had all the attributes of an elite NFL linebacker—tough, quick, smart (he earned a business degree with honors, used complex words like "stimuli," and did the *New York Times* crossword puzzle daily, in ink), and an ability to throw the football.

What was that? Why would a linebacker need to concern himself with throwing the ball? Over his career, Clay flung five laterals after intercepting a pass. The first four were great—as beautiful as Albert Bierstadt paintings. Against the Bengals at the Stadium in 1987, he intercepted a pass and returned it 36 yards, then flipped it to 35-year-old defensive end Carl Hairston, who huffed and puffed 40 yards more. Plays like that can be ill-advisedly habit-forming. But it was his last lateral for which he is most remembered, when Bierstadt suddenly morphed into Salvador Dali.

On December 23, 1989, we were in Houston, hanging on to a 17-13 lead, and the AFC Central lead, with less than five minutes to play. Houston was smarting from a 61-7 shellacking at the hand of the Bengals the week before, a game in which Cincinnati coach Sam Wyche made no secret that he was running up the score. The Oilers had the ball, and Warren Moon was in the shotgun formation. Suddenly the ball was snapped, and Moon wasn't expecting it. It sailed overhead and bounced on the Astroturf. Clay zipped in and scooped up the ball. All he had to do was follow conventional wisdom that is drilled into every kid from the first day of high school freshman football. Fall down and we would be in position to milk away the rest of the clock. But Clay wasn't conventional. He always wanted to make a creative play. But now wasn't the time.

I'm sure Clay remembered the race through the marching band in a game between Stanford and California in 1982. Those are the kind of plays he would dream about. That play took five laterals. This would take just one.

I watched in horror as Clay pirouetted around and tried to fling the ball to defensive tackle Chris Pike, who was just as surprised as anyone as to see the ball coming his way. Clay didn't just try a typical underhanded lateral flip—he tried a semi-jump pass. At 6-7 and 300 pounds, Chris was a hard target to miss, but the throw was off, Chris couldn't react fast enough, and the ball fell back to the turf. Ernest Givins recovered for the Oilers on our 27, giving them new life and new downs. We blitzed the next play, and Moon beat it with a touchdown pass to Drew Hill, putting Houston up, 20-17, with 4:46 left. We had successfully fucked away a 17-point lead.

Our offense then did a most inopportune three-and-out, and we punted with 4:13 left. Now the Oilers were in position to get a first down or two and win the AFC Central for the first time in their history. A holding penalty sent them backward, and Mark Harper busted through on a blitz to sack Moon for an 11-yard loss on third down. It was good to see Moon take a seat. He ripped us for over 400 yards in the air. Our offense would get one more chance.

Enter Kevin Mack. This season had been a series of struggles for the former Clemson Tiger. We were out of timeouts and were 58 yards away. He picked up a 12-yard gain on first down. Then on a critical third down on the Oilers' 15, he banged through for an 11-yard pickup and first down on the 4. Then Kevin took the ball right into the teeth of the Oilers' line and carried three men on his back as he crossed the goal line. That was the greatest 4-yard run I'd seen in all my years of football. That was his only score of the season, but certainly, it was the biggest of the 46 touchdowns in his nine-year career. For the fourth time in five years, we were division champions. A team effort, yes, but in the tight, critical situations we often found ourselves, someone always seemed to find that extra push for which the rest of us were gasping. I can't begin to express the absolute joy of seeing Kevin come through in the clutch so huge. In the locker room afterward, Kevin clutched the ball like a torch of freedom that lit the way into the promised land. He openly wept while Art Modell embraced him in the training room. That was one of those beautiful sights that I, and 50-some other players and coaches, will remember for the rest of our lives. Kevin went on to be the fifth-leading rusher in Browns history.

The Oilers hosted the goddamn Steelers the following week in the AFC wild-card game. Gary Anderson booted a 51-yard field goal in overtime to give the goddamn Steelers a 26-23 win. It was the last game with the Oilers for coach Jerry Glanville and his off-color antics.

When we got back to Cleveland in the wee Christmas Eve morning hours, Clay's '73 Capri wouldn't start. Someone had to give him a jump. The Capri, and the metaphoric meaning behind it, sparked back to life and sailed off into the wintery night. It continued on almost as long as Clay's career—16 seasons with the Browns and three with the Falcons. Making the Pro Bowl five times, he holds the Browns' franchise record for sacks (76.5), and his 279 games over 19 seasons are the most by any linebacker.

Marty Schottenheimer described Clay as "one the top three or four guys I ever had the privilege of coaching." I'll second that, and add that he was one of the top three or four guys I've had the privilege of just knowing.

The 1989 season started off most auspiciously under new head coach Bud Carson despite some preseason difficulties. We opened the exhibition season against the Philadelphia Eagles in London's Wembley Stadium, a facility built in 1923 that was even creakier and quirkier than Cleveland Stadium. That might have been good PR for the league, looking to expand its market of interest into Europe, but it was a bit of a disruptive event for our preseason preparations. Eric Metcalf and Lawyer Tillman were holding out for better contracts, and stayed out the entire exhibition season. Bud switched me to safety, then back to my regular right corner position just before the regular season started. The opener was in dreaded Three Rivers Stadium against those goddamn Steelers, but this was one of the easiest wins in Browns history. We scored defensively three times, forced eight turnovers, and pounded them, 51-0, in a driving rain. The next week, we took it to the Jets, 38-24, on the lakefront. We were scoring and playing defense, and once again, we knew were going to be in for the long haul. But we then lost three of the next four, including a rematch against the goddamn Steelers. Then four more impressive victories, followed by a tie with the Chiefs in Marty Schottenheimer's return to Cleveland. That's when things began to slip away. We lost a Thanksgiving Day game in Detroit, then got beaten by the Bengals and Colts. Then we pulled off an overtime win over the Vikings and wrapped up the division in that Saturday night shootout in Houston.

Our 9-6-1 record got us a bye week in the playoffs. We would host the AFC East champion Buffalo Bills on January 6, 1990. The Bills were dealing with some ongoing behind-the-scenes struggles throughout the year. Every team goes through them to some degree every year, but the Bills' battles were more public, earning them the name "Bickering Bills." Before the season started, Bruce Smith, their outstanding defensive end, tried to sign with Denver, but the Bills matched the offer, which Smith didn't want. Wide receiver Chris Burkett wanted a new contract. Robb Riddick was suspended for a drug violation.

During a *Monday Night Football* loss to Denver, Jim Kelly got into it with Burkett, and Burkett threatened to quit the team if he didn't get his starting job back. The Bills saved him the trouble and cut him two days later. In Week 5, Kelly got hurt in a loss to the Colts and publicly blamed his offensive line, singling out Howard Ballard. The next week, former Bill Greg Bell, who had been sent to the Rams in a trade that in part brought Cornelius Bennett to Buffalo, ripped his former team, accusing Jim Haslett and Fred Smerlas of being "rednecks." He also accused head coach Marv Levy of being a "con artist." Assistant coaches Tom Bresnahan and Nick Nicolau got into a fistfight while the two were reviewing game film in the week leading up to a Week 8 game with Miami. The biggest and most public blowup occurred when starting running back Thurman Thomas, asking to address Jim Kelly's criticism of the offense—and the pass-catching ability of running back Ronnie Harmon in particular—criticized Kelly on a Rochester, New York, television show. When asked what position the Bills could upgrade, Thomas replied, "Quarterback." Thomas first claimed he was just joking, but later, when appearing on Paul Maguire's *Budweiser Sportsline* show, he affirmed that the team didn't appreciate Kelly's public criticism.

Thomas and Kelly later held a joint news conference and apologized to each other and the fans. Somehow, though, despite all the infighting, the Bills were able to put together four consecutive AFC titles beginning in 1990. No team in either conference has topped that.

The temperature dangled in the mid-30s, a relatively balmy day by the lake. The December snows had done a number on the field, which was not much more than green-painted sand. Defensive end Al "Bubba" Baker said we should go out there with beach towels and flip-flops. David Frey, the stadium groundskeeper, hinted at the turf's "lack of grass" and at its not being "perfectly flat."

The Dawg Pound was in full splendor, and the drab creakiness of the old stadium did nothing to impede the incredible electricity. But the Bills tried to short-circuit that electricity with a 72-yard strike from Jim Kelly to Andre Reed in the first quarter. Just like that, we were in a 7-0 hole. But our offense came back with a drive that set up a 45-yard field goal by Matt Bahr. Then in the second quarter, Bernie Kosar, battling a staph infection in his right elbow, flung a deep throw to Webster Slaughter for a 52-yard score and the lead. Kelly then hit 33-year-old James Lofton for a 33-yard score, but Bernie responded with a 3-yarder to tight end Ron Middleton. While there was plenty of back and forth action in the first half, the real drama would be in the second half.

We opened the third quarter with another Bernie-to-Webster strike, this one from 44 yards. That gave us a 10-point lead, and we felt the momentum squaring to our backs. But Kelly kept coming back, and he hit Thurman Thomas for a 6-yarder to cut the margin back to 24-21. It was going to one of those days—our best offensive performance of the year vs. our worst defensive performance of the year. The Browns and Bills would rack up 778 combined yards and 42 first downs.

But now the fireworks began. Eric Metcalf was always as dangerous as a stick of dynamite soaked in gasoline next to a campfire in a stiff breeze. Browns fans remember Eric for his timely big plays, darting through the secondary, turning short passes into long touchdowns, and of course his punt and kickoff returns. His most memorable performance came against the goddamn Steelers in October 1993, when he became the first Brown and only the eighth player in history to return two punts for touchdowns in a game. Eric fielded the kickoff at the 10 and sliced through the right side, kicking on the afterburners and racing untouched for a 90-yard touchdown. Just what we needed.

Yet plenty of drama remained. Scott Norwood banged home a 30-yard field goal in the fourth quarter, countered by Bahr's 47-yarder, keeping our 10-point margin intact. Kelly got to work. He dumped passes to Thomas, who worked his way out of the backfield and into the secondary for big gains. The Bills marched down the field, and with 3:56 to go, Thomas scored on a 3-yarder from Kelly. But Lady Luck, with whom we could never seem to get to first base throughout my nine years with the Browns, was about to show up for a blind date and a couple of long-past-due smooches. Norwood slipped on a patch of icy sand as he tried to kick the extra point toward the west goal and drilled the ball off the ass of one of his offensive linemen. That kept us up, 34-30. Should the Bills get the ball again, they would have to go for the touchdown.

Another three-and-out sequence followed for our offense, and Kelly and Company set up shop on their own 26 with 2:41 remaining. Kelly calmly, coolly and methodically dinked and dunked passes, converting two fourth-down situations along the way.

Browns fans realized they had seen this horror movie before. Kelly was playing out a terrifying remake of "The Drive," starring in the role of John Elway. Kelly then hit a wide-open Ronnie Harmon in the hands in the left side of the end zone, but for whatever reason, Lady Luck delivered a most sweet smooch, and Harmon just plain old dropped it—the ninth dropped pass of the afternoon for the Bills. Maybe Kelly's criticism of Harmon was right. Thomas, keeping with the season-long exchange of barbs among the Bills, later complained that Kelly had just held the ball too long on that play.

"We're not letting these motherfuckers fuck us over," I yelled in the huddle. "Shut these bastards down."

Amid the alternating words of encouragement and vulgarity among ourselves, we called for a man-to-man coverage, which meant Clay was going to have to shadow Thomas, who already had burned us for 150 yards on 13 catches, out of the backfield once again. The Bills came out in a three-receiver formation, with Thomas on the inside. Thomas broke inside, but Clay was playing it perfectly. He intercepted the pass—his first postseason interception and Kelly's 54th throw of the game—on the 1 and slid on his back. He lay there, clutching the prize, looking up into the gray sky, grinning from ear to ear. Felix Wright, Robert Lyons, and Thane Gash hovered over him to make sure he didn't have any sudden creative ideas. After the whistle, he popped up and tossed the ball safely into the stands.

What Clay didn't know is that I was wide open for a lateral. Oh well. Maybe next week.

This turned out to be my last game in fabled Cleveland Stadium. The sweet joy of the moment crowded out the thought in the back of my mind that my days with the Browns perhaps were about to end. At the outset of the year, Bud had wanted to move me to safety, which in retrospect wasn't really a bad idea. In fact, I'd say it was a great idea. That move could actually have extended my career by a couple of years. But the way in which it was handled and turned out left a bad taste in my mouth. So as I returned through the narrow tunnel back to the locker room, I wondered if I would ever walk those planks the other way again. At that moment, we didn't know whether we were going to host the AFC title game against the goddamn Steelers or travel to Denver. The next week, we lost to the Broncos, 37-21, in a drama-free AFC title game, the third time the had Broncos denied us the Super Bowl.

I never scored a touchdown in my NFL career. Had Clay bounced up and lateraled to me, I would have gone out in a blaze of glory.

CHAPTER SIXTEEN

Dawg Gone

Gearing up for the 1989 season, the Browns were assembled in the "war room," doing their annual diligence on whom to draft. Bud Carson had just been hired as head coach, replacing Marty Schottenheimer. Marty had left in what appeared to be a "mutual understanding" after our wild-card playoff loss to Houston in the strange year of 1988. Art Modell wanted to hire an offensive coordinator, but Marty balked. Marty went on to be hired by Kansas City. We drafted 13th that year and picked up Eric Metcalf out of Texas. Eric was a little guy, not as small as Ice Cube McNeil, but his jolting, darting running style would make him the bane of kick return coverage coaches for years. Eric was the only worthwhile pick of the '89 draft.

I signed a new deal with the Browns, collecting $650,000 in 1989, $700,000 in 1990 and $750,000 in 1991.

Frank Minnifield and had I made the Pro Bowl three consecutive years, from 1986 to '88. Yet, during the 1989 training camp, Bud thought that it was somehow a good ploy to tell the media that "there was some slippage" in my play. He couldn't come up with details, just saying, "I'd rather not get him thinking about it."

Yeah, sure, way to ease my mind.

Then came one insult too many. Bud said that Frank "is as good a bump-and-run guy . . . you've got to go back a long time to find one like him. Don't lump those two guys continually in one category. Frank, you've got to go a long way to find better corner than him—anywhere. He's not over the hill."

What? I was now over the hill? Thus was the beginning of the end.

It is true that I missed parts of five games in 1988 with nagging leg and groin injuries. And I did miss the regular-season finale against Houston. Injuries are part of the game—they don't necessarily mean one's talent or desire has somehow diminished. I had started 113 of the 116 games since 1981.

Defensive backfield coach Jed Hughes then told me the news: Bud wanted to move me to free safety and start Tony Blaylock, the Browns' fourth pick of the 1988 draft, at right corner. That wasn't necessarily a bad idea; in fact, I had talked about it for a while. I was anticipating this possibility and was trying to add a few pounds of muscle to better fit the position. But one thing was for sure: No matter where they put me, I needed to be a starter.

This is exactly how Thom Darden had felt during training camp my rookie year, and I couldn't blame him. I knew the game too well and didn't want to spend the end of my career shivering away on a muddy sideline. I knew I still had the speed, the power, the drive, and ambition to play anywhere in the league. If the Browns didn't see that, well fuck 'em.

I didn't want to leave the Browns, I didn't want to leave the community. I was well-rooted in Cleveland, had recently purchased a beautiful home on Lake Road in Bay Village, ran the Top Dawg football camp for kids, and had no desire to tear up stakes and try things out all over again somewhere else. But if it came to that, so be it. I was never a negative force on this team, and no way would I ever be.

In our second exhibition game of the year, against Detroit, I got my first start at free safety. However, I would still have to compete with Felix Wright and Thane Gash. Felix had been the starting free safety since 1987, and he was no slouch. Not only was he quick and tough and could steal passes, he made the best of his chances to return them. In his two years as a starter, he picked off nine passes and returned them for an average of 30.9 yards, a club record. He also was second on the team in tackles in 1988. But moving me to free safety meant bumping Felix, the only Dawg who refused to bark, over to strong safety. Understandably that didn't sit well with Felix. But Felix knew this game was a business, and we remained friends through the awkward situation.

The great safety experiment went bust. Anthony just couldn't play corner. Just before the start of the regular season, Bud switched me back to right corner. I had mentally and physically prepared to play safety and didn't want to make the switch, but Bud realized the whole plot was a mistake, and I wanted to do what I could to help the team.

We had a streaky season in 1989, but we still managed to get to the AFC title game for the third time in my career.

*   *   *

After the 1989 season, I fully believed I still was going to be playing for a couple more years. But it was no surprise when in early February 1990 the Browns released their list of players who were left unprotected by the second year of Plan B free agency. These were mostly older veterans who had the fatter part of their contracts coming due and/or recovering from major injuries. The average age of the 37 protected players was 25.8. The average age on the unprotected list was 28.4. I was on the list, along with 16 others, such as Matt Bahr, Al Baker, Eddie Johnson, Gerald McNeil, and Ozzie Newsome, but it was my name that was in *The Plain Dealer* headline. Under the rules of Plan B, we were free to negotiate with any team for 60 days. Technically, we couldn't return to our current teams until then, but there were plenty of verbal assurances for some players that they were wanted back. The first year of Plan B, the Browns lost 10 of the 21 players they left unprotected. League-wide, 229 players switched teams.

Publicly, the Browns said they wanted me to return, but also publicly made no promises, not that I expected any. Privately, the Browns gave me no wink or nod as to whether they desired my services further. In fact, they told me to give thorough consideration to any offer that came in. I could tell the Browns were passive-aggressively directing me toward the door.

My agent, Bud Holmes, received inquiries from some other teams. The world champion San Francisco 49ers seemed to have the most interest, and Bud and I went out there for a visit. We met with their head coach, George Seifert, and defensive backs coach, Ray Rhodes, who's the defensive backs coach for the Browns now.

I still was determined to keep all of my options open, but then the Browns pulled another move that sealed my fate. During the Plan B signing period, the Browns signed Raymond Clayborn out of New England. I had dinner with him during his visit to Cleveland and knew him from playing against him a few times and alongside him in the Pro Bowl. He was a helluva nice guy, and certainly I couldn't fault him for trying to extend and make the most of the final years of his career. But Raymond was 35 years old, which is about the upper limit of the upper limit for defensive backs (Washington's Darrell Green being the most notable exception. Twenty seasons with the Redskins, and on his 50th birthday, he ran the 40 in 4.43 seconds). Bud had more than hinted that, at 31, I was over the hill. So what a surprise it was when I heard that the Browns had indeed ponied up and signed Raymond, and even more of a surprise that while at the owners' meeting in Orlando, Florida, Bud had named him to my starting right cornerback position four months before training camp was to begin. And this is something I found out by reading it in the paper.

Bud supposedly had tried to call me a few times to break the news, but let's just say I was too busy to take the call. I probably could have handled it a bit more diplomatically, but after being the starter for nine years, I had been disrespected. I just wanted to choke his pudgy ass out. I believe the Browns' organization wanted to keep me but Bud didn't.

In late March 1990, I agreed to a two-year deal with the 49ers. I held a news conference at one of my favorite restaurants, Tony Roma's in North Olmsted, where I also hosted a weekly radio show. With me were Ozzie, Frank, Felix, Mike Oliphant, and Tony Baker. I had a prepared statement. In part, it went like this:

"All of us at one time or another have been offered a change of business address. However, this does not mean we look to change our living home address. My decision to leave the Cleveland Browns after nine years is just that—a business decision, one that was thought about when I was placed on the unprotected list. At first, I was committed to return to my teammates. However, when the world champion San Francisco 49ers call and tell you you can help them in their quest for another Super Bowl, I had to listen. My heart is and always will be in this city, with the people of Cleveland . . . the salary I will make with the 49ers will actually be brought back to the Cleveland economy."

I invited everyone to come out to San Francisco for the Browns-49ers game that would take place in 1990.

After my announcement, the Browns' front office served up the usual obligatory slate of candied departure well wishes. Kevin Byrne, the vice president of public relations, commended my "Pro-Bowl-caliber play, leadership in the locker room, and for being a community volunteer we've been very proud of." Art Modell said, "I'm saddened he's leaving. He has had a key role with the team as a leader for a number of years." Bud said, "I'm not surprised at his decision because I heard it was coming. I hate to lose him. He's been a valuable part of the Browns for a long time." Ernie Accorsi, executive vice president of football operations, said, "We'll miss him most as a leader. He was an All-Pro and has the personality to lead."

Raymond was wasting no time getting ready to take over. He was already working out at our Big Creek Fitness Center just a few hours before my news conference.

I had great hopes for a couple of great years in San Francisco. Leaving the Browns had worked out well for Bob Golic, Lyle Alzado, and Greg Pruitt. Certainly I had enough left that the same could work for me. Ed DeBartolo and Carmen Policy led a first-class organization, and coach George Seifert welcomed me to the fold. Their quarterback coach was Mike Holmgren. During camp, I had to cover the likes of John Taylor and Jerry Rice, who were catching balls thrown by legends Steve Young and Joe Montana. And I would play alongside Ronnie Lott, the great safety who was drafted the same year I was. The 49ers had won two straight Super Bowls and were favored to win a third, and along the way, they had established a record 18 consecutive victories on the road. I saw action in their first exhibition game.

But I never really felt I belonged. My heart just wasn't into it. Two weeks into the exhibition season during practice, I leapt to break up a pass, and I felt a snap and burn in my right quadriceps. I've had pulled groins and strained hamstrings throughout my career, but I could tell this was trouble. It hurt like a sonofabitch. The muscle was torn, and the medical staff recommended surgery as the best way to fix it. That would mean an extensive rehabilitation program. Or I could just let it heal slowly on its own.

I called my wife, Hikia, back in Bay Village. "I think it's time to shut it down," I said. "This leg isn't getting better anytime soon, and I think I just don't have the energy left to fight through this." The money was nice, yes, and I was poised to make the most amount I had ever made in my career. I had picked up a $100,000 signing bonus already. But it didn't mean everything, and I had plenty of business pursuits that could benefit from my full-time attention. I was a partner with Walter Payton in the ownership of 27 nightclubs, and we were looking to expand further.

Hikia agreed, so on August 28, 1990, after starting 129 of 132 games in more than nine seasons, 26 interceptions (putting me ninth on the Browns' all-time list), 440 tackles, 100 passes defended, and three Pro Bowl appearances, I announced my retirement from professional football.

It was another banner year for the 49ers as they went 14-2 in the regular season and made it to the NFC title game. How sweet it would have been to be part of that. Maybe I would have contributed the one or two critical plays the 49ers would have needed to make it to their third straight Super Bowl. We'll never know.

Staying with the Browns would have been agonizing. Despite knocking off the goddamn Steelers in the opener and a sweet last-second *Monday Night* win in Denver, Cleveland's 1990 season was horrible. They were shut out three times, while surrendering 462 points overall, the most any team gave up in one season in the 1990s. Bud Carson was fired midway through the season, and Jim Shofner took over but could eke out only one more win, giving the team a 3-13 record.

No question, I had retired at the right time.

Postscript

One of the blessings of achieving success at the level I did was the fact that I could live just about anywhere I wanted. Just before the 1988 season, Hikia and I purchased a beautiful home on Lake Road in Bay Village. The house stood on a shale cliff overlooking Lake Erie, with magnificent shimmering nighttime vista views of downtown Cleveland. We chose to live in Bay Village for much the same reasons why everyone else there chose to do so—top-notch schools, very low crime, and the leafy beauty of the quiet streets. Several other players past and present lived there, such as Otto Graham and Doug Dieken, and at one time, so did former New York Yankees owner George Steinbrenner.

We were welcomed into the community, and our kids were welcomed in the schools. We enjoyed living in Bay Village, and everyone there was kind and courteous. The people of this small, 7.1-square-mile town were always friendly and welcoming to all of us. Living in Bay (everyone there referred to it just as "Bay") only confirmed what my parents had taught me—a person's color is irrelevant to his character. The people of Bay, like other fine communities, seek the best possible environment for their families, and who gives a damn about your neighbor's color?

*   *   *

Although my marriage to Hikia ended after more than 20 years, I hold no grudge and wish her well. I was a good husband but not perfect.

I have four beautiful kids, all of whom mean the world to me. My oldest, Kyle, came along when I was in college. His mother and I didn't get along too well, but we did the best we could to provide him with the best possible upbringing. He's now an information tech manager for Progressive Insurance and a reservist in the U.S. Army. He's done tours in Afghanistan, Iraq, Saudi Arabia, and Italy.

My oldest daughter, Marva, named after my mother (though we call her Merci) graduated Phi Beta Kappa from Howard University and is teaching school in Phoenix while she pursues her law degree at Arizona State University.

My daughter Hannah, now attending Bowling Green State University, set almost every record in track and volleyball at Westlake High School.

My youngest, Hanford Jr., is now attending Ohio State University and is pursuing a degree in civil engineering. He played football and wrestled at Westlake. An injury kept him from playing most of his senior year. I couldn't stand to watch him wrestle—it was just him and his opponent there on the mat, and there was nothing I could do about it.

Each of these kids has made me a very proud papa.

How I wish my parents were still here to see what these kids have accomplished. I think about my parents a lot. Whenever I speak to a group of young folks, I remind them about the Fifth Commandment—honor your father and mother. Even if you don't always like what they do, you'll miss and appreciate them more when they are no longer around.

*   *   *

Since retiring from football, I've pursued several business interests. After taking some time off to just do nothing, I got into radio and television, hosting talk shows on WTAM radio and working as an analyst for pre- and postgame shows for Browns games on radio and TV. I also did color work for the Arena Football League's Cleveland Gladiators. Most recently I signed on as a regular on ESPN radio 850 in Cleveland as an analyst.

I particularly enjoy working high school football games for Fox Sports Ohio. In 2011, Bob Golic hired me to coach his team in the Lingerie Football League, the Cleveland Crush. Once when I sold my house, I noticed how much the agent earned, and thought that looked like a pretty easy way to make large chunks of cash, so I obtained my real estate license and eventually my broker's license. With my contacts with the Browns' organization, I've done pretty well listing houses for players and coaches.

But my favorite activity still is interacting with the fans. I just love it when a dad comes up to me and says to his 7-year-old son, "This is Hanford Dixon. He's the guy who started the Dawg Pound." Signing an autograph for a kid is at least as big of a thrill for me as it is for that kid. Maybe even more so for me. What an honor, and what a blessing, to be asked for an autograph by a big-eyed 7-year-old. That will never get old.

*   *   *

Football still is and always will be a huge part of my life. I thank God for blessing me with the natural ability to play this great game and to be affiliated with some great people on all levels. If I could physically still play the game, I'd be in the middle of the muck taking down Adrian Peterson or stealing a Ben Roethlisberger pass. Even when I watch replays of old games from years gone by, I still sit on the edge of my seat, living and dying with each play. Despite two hip replacements, I still have 10 plays left in me, as long as I don't have to keep up with any wide receivers. Do you hear that, Coach Shurmur? You've got my number.

Bibliography

Boyer, Mary Schmitt. *Browns Essential: Everything You Need to Know to Be a Real Fan!* Chicago: Triumph Books, 2006.

Browns Media Guides. 1984-1989.

Browns News Illustrated. 1985-1988.

Cleveland Browns: The Official Illustrated History, The. Charlotte: The Sporting News, 1999.

Cleveland Magazine. Various articles from December 1988 and April 1989

Cleveland Plain Dealer. Various articles from 1981-1990.

Cleveland Press. Various articles from 1981.

Clevelandseniors.com. Various pages on various dates.

Cockroft, Don. Interviewed by Randy Nyerges.

Cox, John; sports broadcasting director, University of Southern Mississippi. Interviewed by Randy Nyerges.

Dixon, Debra. Interviewed by Randy Nyerges.

Dixon, Hikia. Interviewed by Randy Nyerges.

Eckhouse, Morris. *Day by Day in Cleveland Browns History.* New York: Leisure Press, 1984.

Friedman, Avery. Interviewed by Randy Nyerges.

Grossi, Tony. *Tales From the Browns Sideline.* Champaign: Sports Publishing, 2004.

Harvey, Sean. *One Moment Changes Everything.* Champaign: Sports Publishing, 2007.

Heaton, Chuck. *Browns Scrapbook.* Cleveland: Gray and Company, 2007.

Henkel, Frank M. *Cleveland Browns History.* Mount Pleasant: Arcadia Publishing, 2005.

Huler, Scott. *On Being Brown.* Cleveland: Gray and Company, 1999.

Keim, John. *Legends by the Lake.* Akron: University of Akron Press, 1999.

Knight, Jonathan. *Classic Browns*. Kent: Kent State University Press, 2008.

Knight, Jonathan. *Sundays In The Pound*. Kent: Kent State University Press, 2006.

Kosar, Bernie Kosar. Interviewed by Randy Nyerges.

Langhorne, Reggie. Interviewed by Randy Nyerges.

Long, Tim. *Browns Memories*. Cleveland: Gray and Company, 1996.

Marva Dixon Funeral program.

Minnifield, Frank. Interviewed by Randy Nyerges.

Mississippi Concurrent Resolution 543, 2005.

Moon, Bob. *The Cleveland Browns—The Great Tradition*. Columbus: SporTradition Publications, 1999.

Newsome, Ozzie. Interviewed by Randy Nyerges.

Pluto, Terry. *Things I've Learned From Watching the Browns*. Cleveland: Gray and Company, 2010.

Rutigliano, Sam. Interviewed by Randy Nyerges.

Rutigliano, Sam. *Pressure*. Nashville: Oliver Nelson Publishers, 1988.

Schafrath, Dick. *Heart of a Mule*. Cleveland: Gray & Company, Publishers, 2006.

Schneider, Russ. *The Best of Cleveland Browns Memories*. Moonlight Publishing, 1999.

Shmelter, Richard. *The Browns, Cleveland's Team*. Champaign: Sports Publishing, 1999.

Tatum, Jack. *Final Confessions of NFL Assassin*. Coal Valley: Quality Sports Publications, 1996.

USM Press Release, October 5, 2010.

Watson, Steve. Interviewed by Randy Nyerges.

About Randy Nyerges

Randy Nyerges is a freelance writer and musician. At age 22 he received his first of several appointments to the staff of the United States Senate, where he wrote speeches and other material for dozens of United States senators and two vice presidents. He graduated with honors from Kent State University with a degree in journalism. He resides in Berea, Ohio, with his wife and three children: Faye, Todd, and Eleanore.